THE MAN WHO TALKED
WITH ANGELS

PASTOR ROLAND BUCK
THE MAN WHO TALKED WITH ANGELS
SHARON WHITE

SonLife International, Inc.
Basking Ridge, New Jersey 07920 USA

Printed in the USA for

G. R. Welch Co. Ltd.
Burlington Ontario, Canada

Daystar
Brisbane, Queensland
Australia

Pastor Roland Buck
THE MAN WHO TALKED WITH ANGELS
Copyright © 1982 by SHARON WHITE
Printed in the United States of America
All rights reserved. No part of ths book may be
reproduced or transmitted in any form or by
any means, electronic or mechanical,
including photocopying, recording or by any
information storage and retrieval system,
without permission in writing from the
Publisher. SonLife International, Inc.
Box 354, Basking Ridge, N.J. 07920 USA
Printed in the United States of America
International Standard Book Number 089221-088-5

Published by SonLife International, Inc.
Box 354 Basking Ridge, N. J. 07920 USA

Distributed in the United States by
NEW LEAF PRESS — HARRISON, ARK. 72601

Simultaneous Printing and Publishing in
the USA for:

G. R. Welch Co Ltd.
Canada

Daystar
Australia

To my wonderful mother, "Charm."

Acknowledgments

Special thanks to Ruth Windom and my sister Marilyn who typed and typed and typed. Also to all of Central Assembly's secretaries: Ricki, Mary, Joyce and Betty for all their help in prayer, typing and encouragement.

To Val and Debbie for the use of the cabin in the pines where a great start on this book was made. To Al and Helen for kid-sitting at a crucial point.

To my husband, Alan, along with my children, Angie and Terry, who joined forces with me in such a beautiful way and made this book possible. They all pitched in with housework and put up with a frazzled mother and wife as she paced and typed and prayed and cried and laughed over the pages of this book.

Contents

The Theme of Pastor Roland Buck's Ministry

I count everything as loss compared to the possession of the priceless privilege—the overwhelming preciousness, the surpassing worth and supreme advantage—of knowing Christ Jesus my Lord, and of progressively becoming more deeply and intimately acquainted with Him, of perceiving and recognizing and understanding Him more fully and clearly. For His sake I have lost everything and consider it all to be mere rubbish (refuse, dregs), in order that I may win (gain) Christ, the Anointed One,

And that I may [actually] be found and known as in Him, not having any (self-achieved) righteousness that can be called my own, based on my obedience to the Law's demands—ritualistic uprightness and [supposed] right standing with God thus acquired—but possessing that [genuine righteousness] which comes through faith in Christ, the Anointed One, the [truly] right standing with God, which comes from God by (saving) faith.

[For my determined purpose is] that I may know Him—that I may progressively become more deeply and intimately acquainted with Him, perceiving and recognizing and understanding [the wonders of His Person] more strongly and more clearly. And that I may in that same way come to know the power outflowing from His resurrection [which it exerts over believers]; and that I may so share His sufferings as to be continually transformed [in spirit into His likeness even] to His death, [in the hope].

That if possible I may attain to the [spiritual and moral] resurrection [that lifts me] out from among the dead [even while in the body].

Not that I have now attained [this ideal] or am already made perfect, but I press on to lay hold of (grasp) and make my own, that for which Christ Jesus, the Messiah, has laid hold of me and made me His own.

I do not consider, brethren, that I have captured and made it my own [yet]; but one thing I do—it is my one aspiration; forgetting what lies behind and straining forward to what lies ahead,

I press on toward the goal to win the [supreme and heavenly] prize to which God in Jesus Christ is calling us upward.

Phil. 3:8–14
The Amplified Bible

PREFACE

Sharon, write a book about your dad! The voice was so distinct that it jerked me awake! I had been half asleep on a plane to Virginia. My mother and I were going to speak and sing at one of the meetings that had been scheduled before dad's death.

I shook my head to clear it and settled right back down to my nap. We had been flying for about five hours. I had been so excited because it was my first long plane trip. I had never been this far across the country. Now the excitement was wearing off. The plane's engines were humming smoothly. It was a beautiful day high above the clouds. I began to drift off again.

Sharon, write a book about your dad! I sat up startled and wide awake! My heart was beating a mile a minute. I had butterflies in my stomach. I knew the voice and it was much louder now. I looked at my mother, who was calmly thumbing through a magazine. All around me the passengers were sleeping or talking softly. This wasn't the first time the Lord had definitely spoken to my heart. As music minister at Central Assembly, I had been awakened in the middle of the night innumerable times as the Lord would speak with me about things I was already thinking about, or He would give me ideas for our musical productions. His speaking to my heart this time was so startling, because writing a book was the furthest thing from my mind.

I thought, "Lord, you know I have tried to write something about my dad since I was in high school, and I've never finished anything. My mind would get so far ahead of my pencil that I would quit in frustration."

My dad and I were very close. I had worked with him as his minister of music for nine years; and being the oldest of four children, I was kind of his experiment, his frustration and his delight. When I was in high school, through college and even a few months before his death, I had tried over and over to write an article about my dad for the *Reader's Digest*. I had planned to send it to the Digest's "My Most Unforgettable Character!" There was absolutely no doubt in my mind that it would be accepted. I could just imagine myself giving it to dad as a Father's Day present. "Oh, by the way, Daddy, there's a little article about you in this *Reader's Digest* you might like to read!" I could just imagine his excitement and pride. But now he was gone, and I thought that this dream had been laid to rest with him.

I reminded the Lord of this and my frustration in writing about Daddy in the past, and the Lord just very simply said, *Get a dictaphone and tell his story.*

Mom and I had a wonderful time in Virginia. I decided not to mention to anyone the way the Lord had spoken to me, not even my husband. That way, if I never did anything about it, nobody could laugh at me.

I returned home, and decided to sleep on my first morning back because I was feeling a little jet lag. I was just dozing off when those butterflies started again, my heart began pounding, and the Lord said, *What about that dictaphone?* "Not now, Lord," I said, "I want to sleep!" No way! I tossed and turned, and over and over in my heart, the Lord kept saying, *Get that dictaphone!* I finally said okay, called a business supply firm, arranged to rent a dictaphone, and immediately fell asleep.

When the young man delivered the dictaphone, I told him I would only need it for a couple of days because I was going to write a book about my father. He looked at me kind of funny, and said, "You're going to write a book in a couple of days?" I said, "Sure!"

To make a long story short, I sat down with the little dictaphone and said, "Okay, Lord, let's go, fill my mouth!" I started telling my story. It took almost ten minutes. I suddenly realized that I didn't have enough information. I said, "Lord, I thought you and I were going to write this book. I thought you were going to speak through me into this dictaphone." I can imagine the Lord smiling, shaking His head, sighing a little, and then He said, just as clear as a bell, *Sharon, make an outline first. I'll help you.* And He did. He impressed me to get information from all the family members and people who had been associated with my father in his growing up years.

As a bonus, my uncle, Paul Williscroft just "happened" to visit from Germany at this time. He had been in the publishing business for many years as part of his missionary outreach. My uncle told me I was on the right track in everything I was doing. He felt the outline was solid, the idea of getting input from family members and friends was great, but I needed to go a step further. He told me I should share with the people in our congregation what I was doing, and get input from them. I told him, "That means I have to tell people, and then I'll be committed to write the book, or really look silly!"

I did share with the congregation, and they were all so excited. Sure enough, people began to ask me every time they saw me, "How's the book coming?" This meant I had to get started. It felt good the day I could truthfully say, "The book is coming along great!"

I knew that my husband Alan, who is an artist, would design the cover. The rest of the book would be just me and the Lord. It was exciting to me to realize that Alan was also a super editor. I didn't have to worry about paragraphs, punctuation or anything that would stop my flow of thought. I could just set my typewriter on fire, and he would take my rough drafts, and put them in good order. We discovered we were really a great team.

As I wrote the last chapter, "Coronation Day," the presence of the Lord so filled my office that I finally had to leave. It took several hours for the tingling in my body and the shakiness in my knees to subside.

One year later, the book that was going to take just a couple days was complete. Writing about my precious father was a special time in my life. Now everyone who reads his book, *Angels on Assignment*, will understand the kind of person he really was. I felt the Lord helping me as I wrote every page. I pray that this book will be a blessing and encouragement to all who read it.

1
WHO WAS ROLAND BUCK?

The stars were still twinkling in the darkness. Soon the first faint light of dawn would streak the skies. Summer was just beginning that early June morning. In downtown Boise, St. Michael's Cathedral bells struck 3 A.M. Here and there the fragrance of the early summer roses was wafted by a slight breeze. As the sound of the bells slowly faded, and all was quiet, Boise slept. What would those sleeping people have said had they known that this day, in the twentieth century, the angel Gabriel would be sent from God to a parsonage on the outskirts of their town, sent to one of their own pastors, with a message directly from the heart of God?

Pastor Roland Buck had pastored in Boise for twenty-nine years. These had been good years, years of steady growth in his church, seeing many people meet Jesus Christ. He was a man solid in his faith. His congregation loved him, his family adored him. He and his wife, Charmian had a beautiful relationship that had grown strong in thirty-six years of marriage.

Pastor Buck was in a deep sleep, enjoying the rest of a man who is at peace with his Creator. Suddenly his sleep was shattered. He was grasped by two giant hands! Although he was an unusually strong man, the grip on his shoulders was so powerful, he couldn't even move. Pastor

Buck's heart was beating like a sledgehammer. Was he awake or asleep? The two strong hands sat him up in bed. Against the faint light coming through the window, he could see the outline of a huge form. A voice boomed out, "Pastor, I have a message for you from the Father. A message that He will help you bring to the whole world!"

In the weeks prior to this, God had really laid the plight of families on Pastor Buck's heart. In his counseling ministry, he noticed that it seemed as if the enemy was trying to get at God by attacking the very foundations of the home. As a result he had been preaching messages on the family, and how much it means to God.

The angel went on, "The Father has noticed your concern, and He is happy with you. He wants you to tell people that He has heard their prayers for their families, and He is sending a host of angels over the whole earth to push, prod, and do whatever is necessary to bring people to a point of accepting Him."

The sun had risen when the angel finally left. He had illuminated many beautiful truths from God's Word to Pastor Buck's heart during this visit. The angel told him to bring the message of God's care to his congregation that Sunday morning.

Pastor Buck had already prepared a good message for his congregation. He shared with his wife what had happened to him. He said to her, "I've been here for twenty-nine years and I have built up credibility in this community. How can I share this?"

He finally decided to wait, and he gave the message he had prepared.

Two weeks passed and, once again, he was awakened by the same big hands sitting him up in bed. "Pastor," the angel said, "you haven't given the message that the Father told you to give!" Pastor Buck said, "Oh, but I will, I will!" He expected the angel to chide with him, but instead he said, "The Father knows how you feel, and He will be with you, and help you to obey Him!"

Pastor Buck then asked the angel, "Who are you?" The angel replied, "I am mentioned in Luke 1:13-19."

Again that night the angel shared with Pastor Buck for many hours about the beautiful nature of God. Both times the angel had been there, pastor was overwhelmed by the presence of God that radiated from him. It was so awesome that he could hardly talk about this experience for some time.

The next morning, Pastor Buck and Charmian looked up the Scripture references that had been given by the angel to let them know who he was. They were overwhelmed as they read Luke 1:19, "I am Gabriel. I stand in the presence of God, and I have been sent to speak to you and to tell you this good news."

That Sunday, Pastor Buck laid his credibility on the line, along with the twenty-nine years he had ministered in Boise, and obeyed God by sharing the message given by divine messenger. It was entitled, "Good News for You and Your Family!"

In the two years that followed, Pastor Buck had twenty-six more visits from the angels. Many of these are described in his book, *Angels on Assignment* as told by him to Charles and Frances Hunter. The last nine visits are shared in this book.

This is the story of the man, Roland Buck, a man chosen by God to bring a message to the world. A message telling of God's love and care. A message letting people know that God is and always will be in control of the affairs of man. Roland Buck was not a mystical person, and he was not super spiritual. He was simply an ordinary man who obeyed God and his obedience led up to that moment of destiny in the wee hours of the morning of June 18, 1978.

Roland Buck was my dad.

My dad was a great storyteller and through the years I had been treated to many stories from his childhood. When I began to research his life for this book; and as his brothers, sisters and friends shared bits and pieces of the memories

17

they had, I was thrilled. I saw the thread of God's presence and direction in his life stretching back before he was born. I began to understand why my father was the kind of person I loved so dearly.

I'm going to step out of the picture in the next few chapters and tell the story of his life before I came on the scene as it was told to me by his family and friends, all wrapped up in the flavor of the many stories he told me about when he was a little boy.

2
AN UNMATCHED PAIR

Roland's parents were definitely an unmatched pair.

Daisy Green, Roland's mother, was born to a wealthy family in England. Her father, William Green, was the captain on the last large English sailing vessel, the *William Tell.* It was a beautiful, sleek vessel, the luxury ship of the line. The *William Tell* catered to royalty, and was also used by the ship's owners. When the ship didn't have royalty on board, Captain Green would take his family with him. By the time Daisy was grown up, she had traveled nearly around the world with her father. She had been around Cape Horn three times. One of the trips had been in winter, an exciting adventure that very few professional sailors of that day had undertaken.

The Greens were well to do. In class-conscious England, they were considered to be in the upper class socially. Daisy's life was one of ease with maids to take care of her every need.

When Captain Green retired, he left England, and moved his family to Vashon Island, near Seattle, Washington.

In America, life for Daisy Green was quite different than what she had been used to in England. There were no more maids, however, the family did have Japanese houseboys.

19

In direct contrast to Daisy, Hoyt Buck was from a very poor family in Missouri. He had gone to school only through the fourth grade.

In spite of his lack of schooling, he was a natural scholar, and read and studied every free minute. He taught himself math and history, as well as some Greek and Latin.

Hoyt Buck was a dashing young man of nineteen when he and Daisy met. He had dark wavy hair, deep blue eyes, and a strong physique from much manual labor. He was the captain of a boat that had been rented for an outing by the church group in which Daisy was involved.

Daisy was very attractive, with long, coal black hair and snapping black eyes. She was barely five feet tall, and had a tiny nineteen-inch waist. She was twenty-five years old. Hoyt took one look at her and decided she was the girl he was going to marry.

Hoyt had quite a task set out for him in winning Daisy for his wife. Her family was against their marriage, because they did not consider Hoyt to be Daisy's social equal. Hoyt courted Daisy, however, and finally persuaded her to marry him.

It wasn't until they went to get their marriage license that Daisy found out that Hoyt was only nineteen. She almost called off the marriage, but he was very good looking, and extremely persuasive. The marriage took place against the wishes of her family.

Hoyt came from a family background that was not religious at all, but about a year before he met Daisy, this determined, strong young man had experienced a real life-changing, born-again conversion. Daisy's family were strong Episcopalians, but she came into a personal relationship with the Lord when she met Hoyt.

Daisy was totally unprepared for the life she was to lead. She had been very sheltered, and was a dreamy romantic. She loved good music and good books. She was a beautiful, flowery writer and in different circumstances, may have become an author. Instead, she entered a life of hardship and poverty without her parents' support. But Daisy Green Buck had met the Lord in a real way, and a faith in Him began to grow, a faith that would sustain her through all the hardships that were ahead. A faith that she implanted in her children along with her love for beauty, her gentleness and her finesse.

Soon after they were married, Hoyt became a lay minister in the Christian church. He worked off and on in the logging camps, and would preach to the men he worked with. In fact, Hoyt never stopped preaching from the time he found the Lord until his death.

And so the stage is dramatically set for Roland's entrance into the world. A totally unmatched pair for parents, but with a deep love for each other and for the Lord.

3
SEVEN BUCKS

It was the beginning of the Great Depression. Times were hard for the Bucks as the children began to arrive.

First came Al Buck, who is now Chairman of the Board for the Buck Knife Company, which is known world wide. The formula for the original Buck Knife was developed by Hoyt's father.

The second child, Gladys, is now a missionary in Germany with her husband Paul Williscroft. They spent two years in Danzig before the war and have been working in Germany and Eastern Europe for the past thirty years. Together they have worked in the Bible school in Germany, established a youth center, started and conducted youth camps, held seminars for Christian workers and pastors and have been heavily involved in literature preparation and distribution for both sides of the Iron Curtain.

Roland always described his sister, Gladys, as a vivacious, sparkling girl, very gracious and feminine, with lots of boyfriends. She used to receive boxes of chocolates, which the younger children loved because she always shared them. In fact, she would promise each of them a chocolate if they would stay out of the way while her boyfriends were visiting!

Then there was Dorothy. "Dot" was a curly-haired tomboy. She was good in sports, and a self-appointed protector of the younger children. She and her husband, the late George Garka, owned a lumber mill in Everett, Washington for many years. The Buck brothers and sisters say that Dot has been the catalyst that has kept the family together by keeping in touch with each one, and planning delightful family reunions. Since her husband's death, this spunky lady has traveled to many foreign lands, and given financial assistance to missionary families as she was able. Dot is not only loved by her own many grandchildren and great grandchildren but wherever she has gone, she has been adopted as "auntie" or "grandma" by the children with whom she has come in contact.

George was next. He is described as being quick-tempered, and would always get into scrapes. George was impulsive and would act without thinking, but inside he had a heart of gold. He was one of his mother's favorites. He became a prominent businessman in California before he retired. He and Roland were very close as youngsters.

The fifth child was Roland, 'Rollie', as he was called then. His brothers and sisters all called him the "angel" of the family , saying he was "too good to live". There was something inborn in him, even then. Something special.

After Roland, came Margaret. She describes herself as kind of a sickly, whiny little girl. Not very pretty, and not very lovable. Roland was her big brother protector, and she literally worshiped him.

Last into the family came Walt Buck. He was a beautiful, dark, curly-haired, little boy, the kind of child that everybody loves. He was the pet of the family. Although he and Roland were four years apart, there was a special relationship between them from the beginning. First, Roland was a loving big brother to little "Wally", as he was called by his family. Then, as they grew up, the two brothers became close friends with a strong bond of love between them. Walt Buck is now the pastor of the First Assembly of God Church in Spokane, Washington.

4
ROLLIE

Roland was born June 13, 1918, in Everett, Washington. He was a large baby, weighing in at twelve pounds! He had curly, white-blond hair and blue eyes. He was a happy baby.

From the time that Roland was a small child, it was evident that God had His hand upon his life. There were many times when he nearly lost his life, but God intervened.

The first time he nearly died, he was two years old. His older brothers and sisters, thinking that they were giving him a treat, fed him some unripe blackberries. Roland became violently ill and began to have convulsions, one right after another. The children all stayed in the carriage house that night, while in the main house the doctor was desperately trying to save his life. It was a long night for the Buck family. The children were so frightened because they were unwittingly responsible.

Morning finally came, and the weary doctor told the waiting family that their little towheaded Rollie was going to live. What a relief! The family was overjoyed. And Rollie basked in the attentions of his brothers and sisters.

The Buck children were soon teasing little Rollie again, as life settled back to normal. He was such an honest, trusting child, it was easy to take advantage of him, and tell him all kinds of tall stories. He soon caught on to their teasing. When he wanted to make sure somebody was telling him the truth, he would look up at them with his big blue eyes, square his dimpled little chin, and tell them to "say honest!" If they did, then he would believe them. His nickname, therefore, when he was small was, "Little Say Honest."

Roland nearly lost his life again when he was about six. He and his older brother, George, loved to climb trees. They lived near the forest and spent many, happy hours playing in the woods.

One day while they were exploring, they found the tallest tree they had ever seen. The two just couldn't resist the challenge. They decided to climb it. They began to climb higher and higher, nearly to the top. Suddenly Roland lost his footing, and fell to the bottom of the tree. He landed squarely on his back, and lay there as though dead. George slowly climbed down. His heart felt like it was beating in his throat. It seemed to take him forever, but he finally reached the bottom of the tree where his little brother lay. "Rollie?" he said softly. There was no reply. Roland lay there so still.

George, only eight, didn't know what to do. He was afraid to go home and tell his parents what had happened, and he was afraid to leave his little brother lying there. So he just sat there watching Roland. The minutes passed, then what seemed like an hour. Suddenly, Roland came to, sat up, shook his head, and said, "What happened?" George was so relieved. His little brother was okay! He told Roland "Let's not tell!" Roland agreed, and the two little boys went home. They never did tell their parents what had happened in the woods.

Although the Buck family was poor, the children didn't know it. Their lives were rich in the things that really mattered. There were many brothers and sisters to play with. They almost always lived near the woods because Hoyt was a logger, so their childhood memories are filled with forests and swimming in the lakes nearby, of the sun sifting through the trees in the lazy, summer afternoons, and the way the

Easter lilies and spring flowers came into bloom. All the different kinds of berries, that when picked and brought to their mother, made the best pies ever eaten, especially those big juicy blackberries! It was Huckleberry Finn and Tom Sawyer all over again. The children made their own rafts and floated in the river, fishing and exploring. There was always something to do in those beautiful times of Roland's early childhood.

There were some bright spots in those depression days. Every once in a while, Daisy would receive a letter from England telling her that one of her wealthy relatives had died and she had received an inheritance from the estate. One of the things the children remember from those more prosperous times was buying big fat oranges.

Roland, in later years, used to make his own kids' mouths water as he would describe peeling one of those oranges, and slowly sinking his teeth into it, letting the juice squirt out so he could savor every bit.

When the children were young, Hoyt developed a serious heart condition. He was concerned because he was the sole support of his family and had to work hard to make ends meet.

One day while he was working in the mill, the pains in his heart became severe. The Lord suddenly spoke to him and said, *Hoyt, I am going to give you a new heart!*

From that time on, he had no more heart pains. Years later when he died of cancer, the doctors told the family that the only thing that had kept him alive, with as much cancer as he had throughout his body, was his exceedingly strong heart.

5
THE FLEAS

Daisy's relatives in England were horrified when they learned that the Buck children were going to public schools. They would have been thoroughly shaken if they had known the circumstances surrounding those school days.

There was little money for clothes for the Bucks, so they dressed very poorly. They weren't alone. During those depression years, there were a lot of people in similar circumstances. There was another problem, however, which made one of their school years miserable.

One of the houses they lived in was infested with fleas. Daisy, a frail, little person, who had never been trained for housekeeping, really had her hands full with so many children, so they all just lived with the fleas. When the Buck children went to school with little red bites all over them, they didn't realize that there was anything socially unacceptable about frankly telling the other children that those were flea bites. Their eyes were opened, when the other children began to tauntingly call them "The Fleas!"

It was a hard year for all of them. Dot made good use of her lunch bucket, defending her little brothers and sisters. She couldn't be with them all the time, but when she was, a lot of kids went home with headaches!

Every once in a while, Roland would come home from school all tattered and torn with a black eye. He never started fights, but he surely defended himself. When his family gave him too much sympathy, he would always say with a twinkle in his eye, "Oh, but you ought to see the other guy!"

Roland often told the following story to depict how Christians could face the enemy or adversity when Christ, as their big brother, was on their side.

There was a bully who loved to torment the smaller boys in the schoolyard and on the bus. He especially picked on little Rollie. One day Roland's older brother, Al, came home from the Navy for a visit. Rollie asked him to ride to school with him. That day, on the bus, Roland went right up to that big bully who had made his life so miserable and kicked him in the shins. He then proceeded to make faces at him, dance around him just out of reach and tease him unmercifully.

The bully could not understand what would make Rollie take his life in his hands this way and, finally, he had had enough. He made a lunge for Roland. Just as he was closing in for the kill, big brother Al stepped into the picture. Al didn't ask questions. He just picked the boy up by the seat of his pants, and left a firm foot print as he kicked him right off the bus.

One of the adventures during Roland's Tom Sawyer youth involved his brother, George, and another friend. George decided that he was going to earn his Boy Scout lifesaving badge, but he didn't want to wait around for somebody to fall in the lake so that he could rescue him. He was pretty sure that would never happen, at least not soon enough for him. He devised a scheme, whereby he and Roland would take an unsuspecting friend who couldn't swim out into the middle of the river on their raft. Then George would push the boy off the raft and jump in to save him. Roland was supposed to verify that George did this. He argued vehemently with George against it, but George's mind was made up. Roland decided he might as well go along with George since he was going to do it anyway.

The day came when George, Roland and the unsuspecting victim took off on a raft down the Pilchuck River. Sure enough, George pushed the boy off the raft at a point in the river he had previously picked out, then he rescued him. They rowed the raft back to shore, but George had such a guilty conscience, he never could claim that lifesaving badge.

On another lazy summer day, George, Roland and another friend decided to row their little handmade raft over to an island, just off Whidbey Island. They were going to camp out for a few days. Halfway between the two islands, they were suddenly surrounded by a school of whales, each about twelve to fourteen feet long.

George was terrified, but Roland showed another trait which he exercised for the rest of his life. He was cool in the face of danger or emergency. He said to his terrified older brother, "Just sit still, ignore them, and they'll probably go away." That wasn't hard advice to follow, because George and the other boy were literally paralyzed with fear. The whales nosed around the raft a little bit, caused it to bounce up and down in the waves, then went on their way.

Times were hard for people everywhere during the Great Depression. There was the winter of the big snows. The water in the Buck's house froze so the family moved into the living room where they could at least be warmed by the fire. They lived on cornmeal mush with skim milk that the neighbors gave them. The following summer Hoyt started a big garden. The vegetables from that garden tasted so good after all that mush.

The Buck family moved to a place with a big apple orchard on one side of the house. The children picked apples in the fall, and put them in sacks. Hoyt would then take them into town and sell them door to door in order to earn money to feed his family.

In 1928 when Roland was ten years old, the whole family came into a real spiritual renewal in an old theater in the town of Snohomish, Washington. Hoyt was a minister in the

Christian church at the time. Neither he, nor anyone in his family, understood the baptism in the Holy Spirit.

The man who had invited Hoyt Buck to special meetings at the theater was an old man named Mr. Yonlik, who worked in the logging camp. Hoyt and Daisy and all the children went to the services every night. Daisy, Gladys and Dot just loved the life and excitement of these meetings, and right away were baptized in the Holy Spirit. Hoyt, however, just could not quite take it all in. He had preached against this for so long. Hoyt gave Mr. Yonlik all the reasons why it was not for today. Mr. Yonlik would just reply, "I can't talk like you can, and I can't argue with you, but I know what I have!"

One Sunday night, a missionary from China was visiting the Christian church. It was a beautiful service and, afterwards, young Roland went to the front to pray. He was literally slain in the Spirit. Nobody in that Christian church had ever seen anything like that before. Then Roland began to speak in a language he had never learned. The missionary was startled, then came and sat beside him. She listened for a moment, then said, "He's speaking in perfect Chinese!" This was the dialect she had learned for her work in China. She began to translate as he was speaking. Roland spoke for over an hour in that language. He told of the mighty wonders of God. God spoke through him, telling these people about heaven and what He was preparing for His people. Roland shared with them in Chinese, translated by the missionary, what God was really like!

Fifty years later in Boise, Idaho, daddy shared with me how the angel Gabriel stood in his living room. He told me the angel was dressed in a white thigh-length tunic laced with gold at the neck, with a wide burnished gold belt at his waist. He wore what looked like white slacks. His shoes looked so bright they were almost like fire. His hair was gold and straight. He was over seven feet tall, and had a slim, but very powerful build. His clothes and face always radiated with a holy brightness because the angel, Gabriel, dwells in the presence of God.

The angel told daddy on this particular visit about that time when, as a ten-year-old boy, he spoke through the Holy Spirit in another language, describing the Father. Gabriel told dad that he was there at that time. He then shared many instances throughout my dad's life when God had sent him to be there. God very definitely had a plan for my dad.

One of the things that God made so clear through His divine messenger, is that God has had a plan for everyone from before the foundation of the world. God let my dad know that events which He has decreed have to happen! People are foreordained. God has included you in His great unfolding plan, but He will not violate your will. You can choose to experience the joy and excitement of being in partnership with Him.

Roland was not perfect. He had a temper and he was stubborn, but these were traits that, after he had been baptized in the Holy Spirit, were redirected. As the fruit of the Spirit began to develop in his life, the stubbornness became stick-to-itiveness and determination to finish something once he started it. His temper, with the Lord's help, became desire to show men the way to reconciliation with the Father. Even as a ten-year-old boy, the compassionate nature of Christ began to stand out.

Another quality which began to surface was a wisdom unusual in one so young. The whole family, especially his brothers and sisters, would look to young Roland as a peacemaker. This was a "fruit of the Spirit" that remained in evidence throughout his forty-one years of ministry. Roland was a peacemaker.

Junior high school days rolled around. The Buck family was still very poor. Their coats were thin and their shoes, when worn through, were lined with cardboard to cover the holes. Sometimes they were lucky in finding an old tire. That was really living, to have some tire tread for the bottoms of their shoes.

Roland was never warm, and in rainy Washington, he was hardly ever dry. They all had to pitch in and work after school to help earn money to keep food on the table. At that time, Roland would work steadily, side by side with his older brothers and his father, never complaining, but always dependable, even when he wasn't feeling well.

When he was fourteen, he developed a severe cold. He kept on working because he was needed. Roland's natural stamina finally gave out, and the cold became double pneumonia, which eventually resulted in inflammatory arthritis.

His fever was so high, and this type of disease produced so much pain on the surface of his skin, that he could not bear to be touched. Night after night, he lay in the living room near the fire suffering terribly with nothing to help the pain.

His little sister Margaret, who loved him so specially, would stay up through the night to keep the fire going. She was the only one he could stand to have touch him. She would bathe his fevered head and body, and keep silent watch over him. She also stayed home from school during the day to help care for him. When Margaret had been sick with rheumatic fever the previous winter, Roland had brought her lessons home from school and helped her with them so she wouldn't get behind. Now it was her turn to do something for her beloved brother.

One night Roland was especially ill. Margaret was keeping her faithful watch by his bed, but she was so sleepy she dozed off. Suddenly she opened her eyes to find that Roland was looking at her. Very feebly, he took her hand, and in a voice so weak it was barely a whisper, he said, "I love you, Margaret!"

Margaret, who was not pretty, who was even kind of bratty, and who got on everyone's nerves, that night felt like she was the most beautiful, special little girl in the whole, wide world. Her big brother loved her.

The Lord brought Roland through with no ill effects, protecting him once again for the special task that lay ahead.

Later that same year, Roland cut his Achilles' tendon very badly. The only way he could walk without pain was to wear one of his sister's high-heeled shoes. So that is just what he did. The other children hooted and laughed at him as he walked to class in his "high heels", but he was comfortable. His foot didn't hurt, he could walk, and in his opinion, that was all that mattered.

Roland went through the first two years of junior high school, and started the ninth grade. Times were so bad and things were so tough for the family, however, that when a job opened up on the night shift at the lumberyard, he decided to quit school and go to work to help support the family. This also gave him the opportunity to send a little money now and then to his brother, George, who was attending Bible college.

Roland's younger brother, Walt, has memories of a compassionate, loving, big brother. When Walt was in grade school, he followed his big brother everywhere. Roland would take Walt with him to the YMCA. Roland loved boxing, and Walt just loved to be with him. Walt says that Roland was such a natural athlete, he could probably have turned professional in several sports. He was a fine pitcher in baseball, good in football, and an excellent boxer. His only problem in the ring was that he was too poor to afford tennis shoes. When he practiced sparring, he would box in his socks. As he would get going, his socks would start to slip off and stretch. They would get longer and longer until soon his opponent would have a real advantage by stepping on his socks, preventing him from moving so fast.

Walt had not accepted the Lord with the rest of his family. One day he came home from school and found no one at home. The whole house was quiet. His mother's clothes were folded on the bed. Walt's first thought was, The Lord has come, and I'm left behind! Then he thought to himself, I'll go out in the woods and see if I can find Roland. If he's still here, I'll be sure the Lord hasn't come yet, because when the Lord comes, I *know* Roland will go! Walt tore into the woods, hollering for Roland.

Roland had been in the woods cutting down some small trees. When he saw his little brother coming, he decided to hide behind a tree and scare him. Roland left his axe sticking in the tree he was chopping. As he watched, he saw Walt frantically looking around. All of a sudden, Walt spotted the axe sticking in the tree. He knew then that the Lord had surely come, taken Roland, and he had been left behind. Walt fell to his knees and began to cry and sob. Then he began to pray at the top of his voice for the Lord to please forgive him and come back and get him too!

Suddenly Walt felt a big arm around his shoulders as Roland gave him a big squeeze. His terror at being left behind receded in the shelter of his brother's bear hug. Walt says that this is how he thinks of his brother, even through the years after they grew up and were both in the ministry. When Walt thinks of Roland, he remembers a strong compassionate arm around his shoulders, giving him a squeeze, that somehow made everything right with the world.

A terrible forest fire had started in the area. Nobody was sure whether or not the houses were going to burn. Roland and George went out to help fight this tremendous fire. It was nighttime and, as they were building backfires up a small mountain road, trees were flaming and falling all around them. Suddenly, they realized they were trapped. The fire had completely surrounded them. There was absolutely no way out. Somehow, and neither man knows quite how, they were able to fight their way through and get out. Neither one was burned at all. Once again God protected Roland.

Hopping a freight train to get where one wanted to go was a common practice in those days. When Roland was sixteen and George was eighteen, they hopped a freight train to Idaho, where they heard there was good work in the potato harvest. It was very cold the night they started their journey and somehow they got separated trying to find a place to keep warm. Throughout the night they walked back and forth on the tops of those freight cars shivering in the cold looking for each other.

The next morning, after traveling several hundred miles, the train stopped in Pocatello. Both boys got off the train, trying to figure out how on earth they were going to find each other. They started walking in opposite directions down the track and practically bumped into each other. Talk about a reunion! This was Roland's introduction to the state where he was to spend most of his adult life.

The two young men were able to earn enough money in that potato harvest to buy their first car. It was an old four-cylinder Dodge. The two brothers really felt as if they had made it as they drove their very own car back to Seattle. As they were driving down the highway, they passed an old couple whose car had broken down. George stopped the car and, being an astute young businessman, said, "I'll tell you what I'll do. I'll push you into the next town for ten dollars."

Roland then exhibited another quality that was to become a trademark of his ministry—a generous heart. He said, "Oh, George, that's too much. Let's do it for five dollars." The couple happily took them up on the offer.

6
THE WOLF TAMER

Although Roland had begun to earn recognition in boxing circles around Everett, Washington, God began to deal with him about full-time ministry. He felt drawn toward Northwest College, although he had not completed high school. All the barriers were removed, however, when he was able to pass a test given by the school that would allow a student to take his high-school and college courses at the same time.

Roland's best friend in college was Walter Daggett, who years later, shares some interesting memories of their college days.

When Roland came to college, he was a strong, curly-haired, young man, good natured, a little bashful around girls, but very friendly. He had a real sincerity in his walk with God, and a faithful spirit. Academically, he exhibited an almost photographic memory.

One afternoon in the dormitory, some of the fellows were trying to study together. It was proving to be almost hopeless because of the joking, wrestling and laughing. Roland glanced at one of the mimeographed sheets, and then casually handed it to Walter saying, "See how much of this I know, Walt." To Walt's amazement, he repeated almost the whole page word for word!

Work was scarce in those days for young men going to college. Roland and Walt really needed to make some money. One day they were wandering around the fishing docks, and came across a man who had a small mountain of old dock timbers and pilings. He was trying to cut them up for wood. Roland and Walt thought, "Here's our chance to help somebody and make a little money!"

They reached an agreement with the man that in the afternoons, evenings, and weekends for the next three weeks, they would saw and split the wood for him. They left the dock in a great state of excitement. They were working men, and they were going to have some cold, hard cash!

For the next three weeks, Roland and Walt really sweated it out down at that old dock. The saw was so ancient it was ready to fall apart. The sparks flew as they worked. No matter how hard they tried, they just could not miss some of the spikes and iron that were deeply embedded in the old timber. Every time they hit iron, they would have to sharpen the saw.

Finally it was over, and the two worn out young men went to collect their hard-earned money. The old man began to figure out how much he owed them. First he deducted the cost of the gasoline, the cost for parts for the saw rig, probably added just a little for his frazzled nerves, and then handed them the grand sum of seven dollars. Divided by two this barely paid for the shoe leather used in walking back and forth from the school to the docks for three weeks.

One thing in Roland's favor was his tremendous physical strength. His reputation as a boxer followed him to Northwest College. There was some boxing at the school, and Roland's strength left his sparring partners feeling like they had been hit by an invisible telephone pole.

A story is told about this mild mannered young "Atlas," who the summer before he started Bible school was working in a sawmill. At one of the noon breaks, one of the fellows started making some remarks about the girls who attended the Pentecostal church in Everett. Roland spoke very quietly to the man, and said, "My mother used to wash our mouths out with soap for talking like that. If you don't quit insulting those girls, maybe you should have *your* mouth washed out the same way!"

The fellow thought this was funny, and kept right on talking, getting even more carried away with his remarks. Suddenly, he felt a strong arm go around his neck in a hammerlock. Before he knew what had happened, Roland had half carried, half dragged him over to the faucet where the men washed up. He grabbed the bar of soap and very calmly and quietly proceeded to wash the talker's mouth out. That day a young high-school boy walked tall in the eyes of his co-workers, many of them twice his age. He had earned their respect.

During his senior year in college, Roland was a proctor for one of the men's dorms. This was a thankless no-pay job as general representative and disciplinarian for the other students. Roland was as full of fun as the next one and thoroughly enjoyed life, but he had been asked to be the proctor because the administration knew they could depend on him.

One day Roland received word that there had been complaints about the high noise level in the dorm, and also quite a bit of concern about the wear and tear on the building and its contents because of the roughhousing that went on.

Roland shared this with the others and things were a lot better for a short time. One day, however, one of the older students started to get noisy and boisterous in the lounge. Roland went over to him with a big smile, and reminded him that he needed to be quieter.

He subsided for a while but finally his good spirits got the better of him. He began carrying on in earnest. Roland spoke to him again in a deceptively quiet voice, "Be quiet, or I'm going to have to take you over my knee, and spank you just like a kid!"

This really set the fellow off. He laughed and made scornful remarks. Suddenly the room got very quiet, except for the laughter of the obnoxious student. His laughter died in his throat as he looked up to see Roland towering above him. Before he knew what was happening, he was grasped by two muscular hands, and although he struggled valiantly, he was forced across Roland's knee. Roland proceeded to give the young man a sound spanking!

The next day Walt came across a cartoon that graphically showed a machine called "The Wolf Tamer!" It was a machine invented by Brer Rabbit, into which he stuffed his old enemy Brer Wolf. The machine beat, shook, kicked, and generally clobbered the wolf. The cartoon showed the wolf exiting in tatters, thoroughly humbled.

Walt cut out the cartoon and hung it in the dorm with Roland's name printed in big letters above it. This became his nickname for the rest of the school year.

Roland thoroughly enjoyed his college days. He was well liked and everyone noted his deep love for God. In fact, although sometimes other people talked about God in a careless manner, Roland throughout his whole life could never speak lightly about the God who meant so much to him. He held God in deep reverence.

When Roland and Walt graduated from Northwest, they decided not to break up their partnership. Roland accepted a church in Granger, Washington. Walt Daggett went home to work for the summer to pay off his school debts. He made plans to join Roland as his assistant in the fall.

7
GRANGER, HOME OF THE SPLASHING DUST

"The dust must be three inches deep here!" Roland was surveying his first pastorate. The sun beat relentlessly down as he unlocked the door of the rickety, old, store building that would serve as his first church. "I've never seen dust that actually splashes!"

The church in Granger had been burdened with many problems through the years, but God had sent the right man, young though he was, to pastor in that tiny town.

As he walked down the aisle of that grimey little building, Roland's heart must have thrilled with excitement. It was small, but it was the beginning of his full-time ministry. Standing in that empty room, he made a commitment to God, a commitment that was to earmark his ministry from that day forth. He told God that his highest priority would be reconciliation between God and man.

During that summer Roland's great physical strength came into the limelight again. He got a job pitching hay to help put food on the table. One day he and the local tough guy, who was considered to be the champion strong man, were on the same crew. Stripped to the waist as they worked, they were an impressive sight. Roland's muscles rippled in the sun as he pitched hay, muscles hardened by years of work in the lumber mills from the time he was old enough to handle a saw.

The friends of the so-called champion began to needle him to wrestle the new preacher. He was reluctant at first. "I don't want to fight a preacher," he said laughingly, but his friends kept teasing him. Finally, the "champ" gave in and said, "How about it, preacher? Want to have a little wrestling match?" Roland politely declined. This, of course, made the other man determined to get the preacher to wrestle! "Hey, preacher, I think I'll just take you over to the irrigation ditch, and duck your head in the water. What do you say to that?" The "champ" was having a real good time harassing Roland. His taunts began to gather steam. Roland breathed a sigh, threw down his pitchfork, and calmly moved over to his challenger. Once again, his coolness, speed, and agility came to his aid. It was soon apparent that Roland had the upper hand, as he easily wrestled the struggling champ over to the ditch, and proceeded to duck *his* head under the water again and again.

This established Roland as the new power king in the Yakima Valley!

In the Fall, Walter Daggett joined Roland as his associate minister. The two young men took turns preaching and leading the song services. Roland was an excellent preacher and spent much time in prayer and meditation over his sermons. Although the congregation was small, Roland's attitude then and throughout his ministry was sharing the kind of Jesus who would leave the thousands of people who followed Him to go to Samaria to minister to just one untouchable woman. To Roland, every sermon he ever preached was the most important, because that sermon might be someone's only glimpse of God.

There were times in those days when Roland sought God, but would not receive any inspiration on what to give his people. He never would give up though, and several times in those early years, he would get right up to the pulpit, and suddenly the power of God would come over him giving him exactly the right sermon to meet the needs of his people.

The two young men did not have much money. During the week they lived on day-old bakery goods which could be purchased for next to nothing. Then Sunday came, the day the ladies in the church invited the young pastors home for dinner. Those dear women loved to cook for them because they were like vacuum cleaners. They ate absolutely everything with such relish; they were fun to feed. Sometimes the two fellows were lucky, and a pie or a pound of butter or even a jar of mayonnaise was delivered to them during the week. Roland used to laugh and tell his children about his co-worker Daggett, who would always divide whatever was brought in half, and say to Roland, "I don't know what you're going to do with your half, but I'm eating my half right now!" God must have definitely kept his hand on those young men with their unusual eating habits.

The blessing of the Lord was indeed upon Roland and Walter in their efforts. In 1941 the church was filled to capacity and they had to build. The two young pastors asked God, "What do we do now? There is no money, but there is no more room!"

As they were driving through town one day, they passed an old apple warehouse that someone had begun to tear down. Roland and Walt looked at each other. "Lumber!" They found the man who owned the building, and offered to help tear it down in exchange for the lumber. The owner agreed to let the men have as much as they needed.

The two young pastors spent the summer pulling nails, and hauling lumber in an old van. They didn't have the slightest idea of how to build a church or any kind of building, but God had even this under control. One of the best carpenters in town came to their church. Each evening he would come by and lay out work for the aspiring young carpenters, so that inexperienced though they were, they were able to get the sprawling frame of that new church up. Not only that, God gives the very best, and the lumber from that warehouse was some of the finest available.

Roland was happy when his young sister, Margaret, moved to Yakima. She had grown up to be a lovely young woman. She was now married, and had become an excellent cook. She was concerned about the eating habits of her brother and his associate, so whenever she could she would invite them over for a delicious home-cooked meal.

One day she decided she would give the boys a real treat. She told them to buy anything they wanted for dinner and she would prepare it for them. Roland and Walt came to her house loaded down with the ingredients for banana cream pies. Margaret laughed and said, "All right, I'll bake your pies, but where are the rest of the things for your special dinner?" Very earnestly Roland told her, "We are used to eating only one thing at a time, and all we want is banana cream pie!" The boys firmly believed that they were in heaven as they settled down to their dinner of as much banana cream pie as they could eat!

Although Roland was a busy young pastor, he kept in close contact with his younger brother, Walt. Walt was now an extremely good-looking teenager. There was a beautiful relationship between the two brothers. Walt had a charismatic personality and was well liked. However, during his teen years a little distance may have come between him and the Lord.

Roland was very happy when Walt told him that he was going to go to Northwest College and then into the ministry. One night about midnight just after he had gone to bed, there was a knock on the door of Roland's little apartment behind the church. He answered the door to find Troy, Margaret's husband, standing there. Troy told him that he and Margaret were very concerned. Walt had changed his mind about going to Northwest, and was instead planning to seek his fortune in California. His bags were all packed, and he was planning to get up early and leave. Roland hurriedly dressed, and drove all night from Granger to Everett. He arrived there early in the morning and walked into Walt's room. Walt eyed him suspiciously, and said, "Rol, what are you doing here?" With a wisdom that was not his own, Roland answered, "Since this is your first day at my old school, I drove all night so I could go with you and help you enroll!" There was a little silence, then Walt said, "Hey Rol, that's great. My bags are all packed!"

This must have been a special day in heaven, as God looked down and watched this choice young man who, through love for his older brother, was guided into a ministry that has affected the lives of many people.

War is Declared! Uncle Sam wants you! Walter Daggett and Roland were busy working for the Lord, and weren't too worried about the draft. Then one day, Walter got an unexpected letter from Roland's mother. She said, "Dear Walter, I hear you are going to be drafted into the army, and as I have been holding you up before the Lord, He gave me this special Scripture to give you. 'He shall give his angels charge over thee, to keep thee in all thy ways'" (Ps. 91:11). Walter had no idea of going into the army, at least not yet, but he thought it was nice of Roland's mother to care. The next day, a draft notice came for him. Reluctantly he said goodbye to Roland, and to the work they had started together.

Roland was left to carry on. It seemed lonely as he walked into his tiny apartment. That loneliness was tempered by the fact that a young lady he had met in Bible school was coming soon to marry him. He was about to start a new era in his life.

The people in his church were so excited about their pastor's new bride. They all got together, and filled up the larder in the little kitchen.

Then they decided that it was a disgrace that their pastor didn't have a new suit for his wedding. They also decided that he badly needed a new pair of shoes. Since Roland took a size 13D, he had a hard time finding them.

Everything was in readiness for the new bride. Then word came. She was not coming. She had changed her mind about marrying him! His heart was broken.

There he was, young Pastor Buck, with his new shoes, his

new wedding suit, a house full of food, and no bride. But God was in this also. It wasn't too much later that a beautiful, spunky redhead with a peaches-and-cream complexion and turquoise eyes came bursting into his life.

8
CHARM

One day there was a knock on Margaret's door. She opened it to find two smiling girls who introduced themselves as the "Sunday school girls." They were going door to door inviting children and their parents to the little neighborhood church they were starting. One of the girls had red-gold hair, and unusual turquoise eyes. She simply bounced with life and sparkle. She had a very unique name, Charmian, "Charm, for short," she said. The other girl whose name was Doris Johnson, was also very pleasant.

Margaret and Troy were impressed with the girls, and decided to visit their church. They loved it. The presence of the Lord was so real.

The more Margaret got to know Charm, the more she thought her name suited her, and the more she wanted to introduce her to her brother Roland.

Thirty-eight years later, Charmian shares a little of her life with Roland.

"One day coming back from the airport, having ministered in another city, I felt the loneliness of my husband being gone. Tears began to fill my eyes and there was an ache in my heart. I was suddenly brought to the realization that I cannot mourn, but I must thank the Lord for allowing me to

46

share thirty-seven good years with a very special man.

"Looking back through those years of marriage, they have telescoped into a moment of time, too short at the very best.

"My girl friend Doris Johnson and I were pastoring a church in the Fairmont community, five miles south of Everett, Washington.

"One lady evangelist was very concerned about us being tucked away in a small community and encouraged us to make 'contacts.' Surely no young men would find us in this obscure area of ministry! How beautiful it is when we give our lives to the Lord. He takes care of us in every way without manipulation on our part!

"My sister-in-law, Margaret Ward, saw a potential of mutual friendship with her brother and I, so she invited Doris and me and her brother to dinner. I was very impressed with this handsome, broad-shouldered, muscular young man named Roland Buck.

"Because he was 'baching it,' he didn't eat very much at home so when he was invited to dinner, he made up for lost time! I mentioned to Doris, "I pity the woman who has to cook for him!"

"The next day he called and asked me to go to some special meetings in Marysville, Washington. It was difficult to get dressed for that date with such a special young man.

"Our courtship was very limited because we had a whole mountain range between us. We were both busy pastoring our own churches and to top it off, this was the time when gasoline was rationed. However, the letters flew back and forth between us.

"I'll never forget the day at convention in Walla Walla, Washington, when Roland took me to a beautiful park shaded with low-hanging weeping willows. On the stream going through the park swans were gracefully swimming. What a romantic setting! He picked out a secluded bench and there in the stillness of a warm spring afternoon he told me he loved me and asked me to be his wife. My heart overflowed with love for him and to God for allowing me to link my life with one so precious. Our hearts beat as one as we shared our dreams and desires for the future.

"The wedding date was set for June 13 which was also Roland's birthday. We were united in marriage in Seattle, Washington, at Fremont Tabernacle which is now Westminster Assembly of God.

"Everything happened so quickly that Roland had not given any thought to where we were going to stay on our wedding night so after the wedding festivities were over we went from motel to motel trying to find a place to stay. Finally we decided to start out in the direction of our honeymoon trip along the Oregon coast. We drove until four o'clock in the morning and had to stay in a rickety motel with creaky floors and leaky faucets. It was so old it almost swayed in the breeze. But we didn't care. We were so much in love. Our trip along the winding roads of the Oregon coast was wonderful as we continued to make exciting new discoveries about one another.

"Our first pastorate together was Union Gap, Washington. We arrived there with our Model A and Rol's brother Walt's Model A loaded with wedding gifts and our belongings.

"Rentals were very hard to find in those days, but as we entered the little town we saw a group of houses that looked like rentals. When we stopped to talk to the owner, he told us we could rent one and work out our rent by taking care of the others.

"The one we moved into was really a shack, but we had a roof over our heads! I cleaned and scrubbed thoroughly, set out our many beautiful wedding gifts, and the little shack began to look like home. Material surroundings didn't seem that important because we had our strong love for each other all wrapped up with the love of God. What else did we need?

"Many times during the winter Roland had to worm his way under the houses, killing multitudes of black widow spiders, to thaw out the pipes or do some repairs. As different ones of the houses that were better than ours became empty we would paint and clean and move in. During the first year of marriage it seemed as though I was continually painting, cleaning, packing and unpacking!

"Finally an attractive little cottage became available which we were able to rent and later purchase for the church parsonage. This cottage was so much nicer than all the others. I almost felt like I was in heaven, or at least very close.

"Our time in Union Gap was such a special time of learning to blend our lives together in ministry to others. Many speak of difficult adjustments their first years of marriage, but I'm happy to say we did not have that problem. Our lives flowed together naturally as we had one main purpose—to build the kingdom of God."

9
MINISTRY UNFOLDING

Finally, I get to join the story. Mother and dad had been very happily married for ten months when I joined them. Daddy used to laugh about really "hitting the jackpot" when I was born. He was so excited about his little girl that as soon as he could leave my mother, he ran to a pay phone in the hospital to let everybody know that he was a father. He had finished making his calls and was leaving the phone booth when the phone began to make a strange noise. Suddenly all the change came pouring out of the coin return, piling up on the floor. Daddy was so excited about the baby that he just closed the door and ran back to my mother's room. He always wondered what the next person to use the phone thought when they opened the door to the phone booth and saw all that change lying there. Daddy picked out the name for his new little girl. He called me Sharon Rose after the Rose of Sharon.

The Bucks moved from Granger to Union Gap, Washington. This was a pretty little town on the outskirts of Yakima. It was nestled in the area of Washington that is famous for its apples.

Daddy spent many hours visiting in that little town. Because of all the fruit, there were many Mexican labor camps full of transient workers. Mother used to laugh at my father and tease him about beating the Welcome Wagon to new people in town.

Union Gap was also near an Indian reservation, and daddy used to take me with him when he held services there. I learned how to sing when I was eighteen months old, but I looked like a much younger child because I was as bald as a billiard ball! It used to really amaze the Indians to see this little bald baby sing clear as a bell, "Jesus Loves Me" and other favorite children's choruses.

God once again honored daddy's hard work and dedication. Soon the little church in Union Gap was filled and it was time to build once more.

My parents told me later that they wondered at the time about spending so much of their efforts with the migrant workers who could not be permanent members of their little church, but it was worth it. Those dear Spanish people got saved, then they would take the message of God's love with them. Years later, mother and daddy reaped the reward of their efforts when they heard reports that many of these people were still serving the Lord.

My father's priority, and now my mother's, continued to be the message of reconciliation.

One day when I was three years old, my Aunt Margaret took me home with her for a visit. I was very happy about the visit, because I had a little cousin, Dick, just my age. We two three year olds had a great time playing together. Unfortunately, on this visit, Dick had a little gift for me—a rip roaring case of the mumps! Margaret had her hands full with two mumpy little cousins.

The visit was a little longer than expected, however, because little Charm was born, and I could not go home until my mumps were gone. I was so excited about having a baby sister that as soon as I arrived home from Aunt Margaret's house, I broke out into the measles, which were promptly passed on to my new little sister. Daddy came home from an evangelistic meeting to find all three of his girls in bed.

The little Buck family had been in Union Gap for four years when the Lord directed them to Gooding, Idaho, a little farming town about one-hundred miles from Boise.

There were two churches in Gooding. One was the little church that had been started in temporary quarters, with a small apartment in the back for the minister and his family. Sitting right next to it was the skeleton of a larger church that had been started, but somehow had never been completed. The frame for that new church had been sitting there for twelve years.

In Gooding, growth occurred once again as my parents rolled up their sleeves. My father could not stand the sight of that unfinished building. With faith burning in his heart, he inspired the congregation to catch the vision for souls and together they tackled that unfinished church. They were so proud of the lovely new facility when it was completed.

Since little Charm was only one, and there was another baby on the way, daddy took his little Sharon everywhere with him. I would ride with him on his visits to members of the congregation with my hand on his shoulder, or sit on my knees beside him with my arm around his neck. I was so proud of my handsome daddy. I would look up at him and ask, "Do you think people will think you're my boyfriend?"

Daddy loved to show off our feats of daring. He would put his hand on the ground, and have me stand on it, then very slowly he would raise his hand above his head with me standing stiff-legged with my arms outstretched. He also loved to show visiting ministers and evangelists how fast he was with his fists, by standing me in front of him. He would jab with his fists, and come within a hairsbreadth of my little nose. What control! I would stand there with perfect trust not even blinking an eye.

Polio, that dreaded disease, hit with epidemic force. Children were falling victim everywhere. I became very ill. My legs hurt so badly I couldn't move without screaming. My fever was high, and my head hurt. The doctor shook his head and said to my parents, "It doesn't look good. It could be polio. You'll have to take her to the hospital in Boise for tests."

Daddy bundled me up in some blankets, and a member of the congregation drove us to Boise. Once again daddy's tremendous strength and stamina surfaced as he held his little girl in his arms. The slightest movement caused great pain to my legs, so the car had to be driven very slowly. Daddy sat in one position, holding me very still for almost three hours.

I was in isolation in the hospital, but all the tests for polio came back negative. Instead, it was rheumatic fever. My legs wouldn't be crippled, but my heart had been damaged. The only cure was for me to lie flat on my back in bed until my heart healed. What a sentence for an active four year old!

Being sick in bed wasn't so bad after all, because daddy decided to teach me how to read. He didn't like the "Dick and Jane" books, so he proceeded to find one that would be more interesting. The exciting little book that he found was entitled *The Saggy Baggy Elephant*. Some of my very first vocabulary words were, "the Limpopo River".

It's a boy! Once again, daddy was busy telephoning everyone with the good news. Little Terry Lee. He was dark like my father, with brown shoebutton eyes. Life was good. I was on the mend, little Charm was a cute ray of sunshine, and now the Buck family had been blessed with a boy!

Six months passed. It was a sunny spring day in Gooding. In the parsonage, mother had her day planned. She was going to whisk through the house and get it all shiny clean for daddy. She got all of us ready for the day, and then about mid-morning, put Terry down for his nap. He was a little fussy, but was probably teething. Mother decided to just let him fuss until he went to sleep. Lunchtime came and she fixed lunch for us girls. Terry was surely taking a long nap. That was good; he'd be really happy when daddy came home.

Daddy arrived and Terry was still sleeping. Finally, mother decided that he had slept long enough. She went into the bedroom to wake up her precious little boy. She picked him up.

Suddenly, I heard mother cry out, "Roland!" She came running into the living room holding their little son out to him. "Roland, he's dead, he's dead!" she sobbed.

Daddy took his little boy in his arms, put him over his shoulder and began to walk with him, patting him gently on the back. He noticed that I was sitting up in bed staring out of my door! He gave me a big smile and quietly shut the door of my bedroom. Not really understanding what was happening, I continued to watch through the keyhole. I had never seen my daddy look so sad.

Carefully, he laid Terry on the couch and called the doctor. The doctor examined the little body, then said gently, "It looks like crib death. We don't know why or how it happens, but there is nothing you can do to prevent it!" Very compassionately he said to my mother, "It wasn't your fault, Mrs. Buck. There is absolutely nothing you could have done".

It was a very hard time for the Buck family. Mother's nerves could not stand the strain. My father took her home to be with her mother for a short while. We two girls were sent to stay with friends. Mother says now that it was daddy's gentleness, love and understanding that brought her through this hard time.

Daddy was only twenty-nine years old, I was in bed flat on my back, his only son had died, mother was ill, when tragedy struck again. His father, Hoyt, died of cancer, and just a short time later, his mother passed away.

What a training time for a young pastor. One day I came to him and climbed up into his lap.

"Daddy", I said, "I'm going to make mommy smile again! I've got a wonderful surprise coming tomorrow morning."

"What is it, honey?" he asked.

"I just asked God to give Terry back to us. I told Him to put him in my bed, and tomorrow morning, I'm going to carry him in to mommy!"

Daddy just hugged me close. Then he told me something I never forgot, a truth that was the foundation stone of his own personal ministry.

"Honey, God can see ahead to what we can't see. He probably looked ahead in Terry's life, and saw some hurt, or maybe He saw that when Terry got older, he might not serve Him. Anyway, God decided that He would take Terry home to heaven with Him right now, and spare him those things that may be in the future. And, honey, I want to tell you something. God always does the right thing. You can trust Him!"

Instead of feeling any bitterness toward God, daddy squared his shoulders and declared that he was serving God because of who He was, not because of what He did. This hard time in his life mellowed him and gave him a depth of compassion for people who were hurting that was very unusual for one so young.

Bible school at midnight? My father was not adverse to trying something new to get out the message of God's love. Mr. Wilbur ("Boom") Slagel had just found the Lord through my parents' ministry in Gooding. He immediately felt the call of God on his life, but he didn't have any formal training. He knew that with his large family it would be impossible for him to go to Bible school to prepare himself for full-time service.

He shared this with daddy, and he could hardly believe his ears when my father said, "That's no problem at all. I'll train you." Brother Slagel said, "But Pastor Buck, I work nights and, as a result, I sleep during the day." Daddy told him, "You come to my house every night at midnight during your lunch break, and I'll teach you from the Bible everything I have learned. This will be your Bible school."

So for the next few months, six nights a week, a young pastor would roll out of his bed at twelve o'clock each night and give the older man a Bible study. This went on until Brother Slagel was ready to go out and pastor on his own.

Pastor Slagel shared the same beautiful knowledge of the nature of God that his teacher had, and pioneered at least four different churches around the country before his death.

Bob Slagel, Boom Slagel's son, was about fifteen. He was the ring leader of the street gang in Gooding. Bob would bring his gang to church, and if he didn't like what was happening, he would get up and walk out, followed by the others.

One Sunday night after the service, the people had gathered in the front of the sanctuary and were having a wonderful time of prayer. Bob was in the back of the church with his friends causing a ruckus. Daddy came quietly up behind Bob, scooped him up around the middle, and literally carried him up to the front and placed him right in the center of that prayer circle. He looked at dad, his eyes flashing with hate, but his hate was totally melted by the great big warm smile that shone back at him.

Several weeks later on a sunny afternoon, as daddy was out driving, he saw Bob with three of his buddies. He stopped and asked, "How about going for a ride with me in my V-12 Zephyr?" This car was a Lincoln and very special. Most cars only had eight cylinders, this car had twelve. Everyone was really impressed with it, especially the boys.

They all hopped in and took off for a drive in the country. They were having a great time when suddenly daddy turned into the cemetery. They all wondered what on earth Pastor Buck was doing there!

Daddy turned to them and said, "Would you mind stopping by Terry's grave with me for a minute?" Of course, they couldn't say no.

As they stood around the little grave in which their pastor's only son had been buried about two months before, dad said to them, "Would you guys mind kneeling here with me for a minute? I would like to have a word of prayer."

They all knelt and daddy began to pray right out of his heart, just talking to God as though he was talking to any one of his friends. He said, "I understand what you are doing in the lives of these boys, but Father, I really do not understand about Terry. Yet Father, I know that you have all wisdom, and I thank you for that. Father, Charm and I dedicated Terry to you, and in your foreknowledge, you knew that somehow his little life would make an impact, even though it was so very short. God, these guys are like my sons, and I would like to ask you today to help them take Terry's place since Terry is with you. God, in this way, Terry's death will not be in vain."

Years later, as Bob was sharing this scene with me to include in my book, he was overcome with emotion as he recalled this event that changed his life.

Bob told me that everyone of the four young men were so broken up, they wept and wept. That day, each of them made a commitment to the Lord that has lasted to this day.

Two of them went into the full-time ministry. Bob Slagel was one of them, and he has been instrumental in leading many people to Jesus. This all began at the grave of a six-month-old boy whose life, though short, *did* count.

10
BOISE

The congregation in Gooding was thriving. The church building had been completed, and the entire community was aware that something was happening there.

The Buck family had survived the storms of adversity and my parents had come through stronger than ever. The Lord had healed my heart and I was able to start first grade right on time. My little sister, Charm, at two, was a happy little girl who had developed an amazing aptitude for putting together any kind of puzzle. Daddy had a wonderful time showing off her ability to his friends. He was firmly convinced that both of his daughters were exceptional.

"Roland! Telephone! It's long distance from Boise!" Mother handed the phone to him, wondering who on earth would be calling.

It was a representative from a little pioneer church in Boise. Reverend Boutwell had gathered together a group of people; God had blessed; and the congregation had built a very small sanctuary in one of the older residential sections of the town. The congregation was much smaller than the one in Gooding.

Reverend Boutwell was moving on to pioneer another work, and the people wanted daddy to come and speak to them with the possibility of his taking the pastorate. As he hung up, he felt a quickening in his heart in response to the invitation. Mother shared his feeling.

Just a few weeks later, my father tearfully preached his farewell sermon in Gooding. He felt strongly that God was moving him to Boise, and that he must obey.

The little church in Boise was called Bethel Assembly of God. They didn't have a parsonage, so daddy purchased a big, sprawling, old house for an unbelievably low price. The people in the congregation banded together and scrubbed and painted to help make this house presentable.

As Mother went through the house, she immediately began thinking, "If Roland will tear out this wall and move the stairway . . . oh, and the living room is so big that adding a wall could make another bedroom!" Daddy just smiled as mother enthusiastically told him all her ideas. He knew that she had a special gift of transforming any place, no matter how drab it might look in the beginning, into a comfortable, attractive home. He was proud of this talent in her and was willing to work with her to accomplish their ideas.

One of the first things he did was put himself on a very small salary. Up to that time, the pastor received the entire Sunday offerings. Daddy felt there must be some money from the offerings to put back into the operation and growth of the church. When he went on a salary, the offerings immediately increased, as people realized that much of what they gave would go right back into the church. The second thing he did was buy an old school bus and he began going door to door inviting boys and girls, moms and dads, to fill it up.

The following was excerpted from a letter from one of those Sunday school kids.

"I first met Roland Buck when I was nine years old. My mother, my two older brothers, my younger sister and I lived in one of the two major ghetto areas in Boise. We were one of the poorest families. The house we lived in was truly a "tarpaper" shack. There were curtains rather than doors between the rooms, no screens on the windows, and in the winter we pushed a rug against the outside door in an effort to keep out the cold. The oil stove that stood in the front room was not adequate for heating a house even this small.

"It didn't seem as if many people cared about the poor people in those days of 1951. I don't remember many people coming to our door. Pastor Buck was the exception.

"My oldest brother Robert had met Roland somewhere in the streets. I sometimes think that Pastor Buck drove through the poor parts of town, looking for people who needed a friend. I was very young then, and could not fully appreciate the depth of caring that motivated a man like him. He gave Robert a ride home. I wonder now what he thought as he entered and surveyed that hovel that we called home. What I do know is that from that Sunday morning on, he picked our family up for church and brought us back home. It wasn't just Sunday mornings that he took on the responsibility for us, but Sunday evenings, Wednesday evenings, and any time there was a special service in town or out of town.

"At the Christmas program there was always a bag of oranges, nuts, and candy for the kids at the church. I wonder how many of those people ever realized that this was just about all some of those children ever got?

"Life separated us, and I went to live with my father. The years passed. I thank Pastor Buck for many things. I thank God that before he was taken home, Roland Buck knew how very, very much I appreciated his efforts above and beyond what many ministers would have construed as their duty. I thank God that Pastor Buck was a man who was willing to go that extra mile. Also that he was a man who went out eagerly into the highways and byways to bring people in. In short, Pastor Buck lived the message he preached!"

Another charter member, Grace Schofield, writes, "Pastor Buck was more than a pastor. He was our friend and brother. In the twenty-five years we had the privilege of sitting under his ministry, we found him to be consistent in his trust and faith in the Lord. He never went from right to left on anything but stayed in the middle of the road. You knew you could trust him.

"He was a pastor who cared about people. When we first came to Boise, the church was on 21st and Alturas. He would go from door to door inviting people to church. Sunday mornings he went picking up children and even washing faces.

"Pastor took our boys out into the country and taught them about cars and driving them. He also helped with school work. When the boys were older and doing their own thing, he held them up in prayer. One Sunday night they both came to church. Pastor told us later that he could see no one but our two boys no matter where he looked.

"When someone came with a need, he didn't just pray, but reached into his pocket and handed them a five-dollar bill or more.

"Pastor was human, he made his mistakes, but was always quick to say he was sorry. There were times through the years that I did not totally agree with him, but I always respected him. We could always go to him and talk things out.

"It was beautiful to see the gifts of the Spirit in evidence in his life. It was no surprise to us that the angels were sent to him. The Lord had trusted him with information throughout the years and knew He could trust him to tell only what He wanted told. He never got puffed up over these things. He was in awe at seeing and talking to angels, but he never felt that it was because he was special. He always included the whole congregation as a family in the visitations. We all felt involved.

"Most of all, he taught us to trust the Lord completely in all things."

With this kind of caring, it wasn't long until the little church on 21st and Alturas was filled to capacity. The congregation pitched in and expanded it as much as possible, but finally it was time to build.

Daddy and some of his board members flew in a small plane over the city and, from high over the town, they found a spot that looked as if it must be right in the middle of Boise. After they landed, they found to their excitement that the spot they had seen was indeed available.

The project for the new church on Latah Street was huge financially in the eyes of the little congregation but, led by their pastor, they plunged ahead. This new church was truly a step of faith, because the building payment per month was as much as the entire monthly budget of the Alturas church.

Because of the more central location, the name of the church was changed from Bethel Assembly to Central Assembly. A lot of people got a real chuckle out of a picture that was run in the local newspaper. A reporter had taken a picture of the tiny storage shed on the site, with a sign on it almost as big as the shed that said, "Future Home of Central Assembly!"

On February 8, 1951, we all were thrilled by the birth of another boy. He was a big baby, weighing in at over ten pounds and was twenty-four inches long. He was named Ted Alan Buck. Daddy teased me telling me that my new little brother was so big that he would probably walk in when he came home from the hospital. I cried because I was looking forward to having a *little* baby brother. I was so relieved when my mother came home with a real baby.

Ted was the hungriest baby anybody had ever seen. By the time he was six months old, he weighed thirty pounds. He didn't stay a baby for very long.

He seemed special to the whole family, his sisters included, possibly because their first little brother was in heaven. He was loved and was the apple of his daddy's eye.

Teddy took my place riding with daddy, an arm on his shoulder and I didn't even mind. As soon as he was old enough, he went everywhere with his daddy.

Dad decided that as long as I had learned to read at four, he would see how Ted could do at two. So Ted, to the amazement and applause of his adoring family, did just that. When he was three, dad took him to get his first library card. The librarian saw him looking at the first and second grade books and said, "Sonny, these are the books you want, the ones with the pictures." Ted very politely told her, "I don't want the books with the pictures, I want the books with the words! I can read." The librarian smiled and probably thought, "Sure you can!" She was still unconvinced and picked a book off the shelf and gave it to Ted. He promptly read the first few paragraphs to her. She was thoroughly amazed and let him have his first library card.

Daddy had a passion for cars, especially old ones, and as he and Ted were visiting and riding around, he began to teach Ted the names of all the cars. At the age of two, Ted could name every car on the road of any year, even though he had a hard time pronouncing the names of some of them. Daddy had fun showing off his son to astonished visitors.

Two years after Ted was born, another little sister was added to the family. Daddy again teased me and my sister, Charm, by telling us that Marilyn was as red as a pair of bright scarlet curtains that he saw hanging in the house we were staying in while mother was in the hospital. Again, we were relieved when our little baby sister, though slightly redder than most babies, was not the color of those scarlet curtains.

It was an exciting day in 1957 when the congregation of about 200 took possession of our new facility. The auditorium could seat 400 and the unfinished balcony would hold about 200 more.

There weren't any pews that first Sunday, just folding chairs. The congregation had plenty of elbow room, but suddenly the dynamic presence of the Lord filled every nook and cranny of that auditorium. The congregation was not aware of the fact that their pastor, as the church was being built, had walked around the site, and prayed over every inch of space. The building was consecrated to the work of the Lord long before it was ever completed.

Since daddy had not taken any increase in salary through the years in order to help make sure the new building was completed, he was faced with the fact that his family had grown, prices had gone up, but he was making the same amount of money. To help make ends meet, he put ads in the paper for remodeling houses and painting, inside and out. He would also buy an old car, fix it up, and sell it for a profit. He was a very busy man. He did pretty well, except when he would come home from a painting job to find a call waiting for him to go to the hospital or to see someone. He would then have to quickly change his work clothes, do his visiting, come back and change again. He felt during those years that he did nothing but change clothes.

He finally decided that it would be less time consuming, and also cut out the constant round of changing clothes to go into real estate as a sideline. Once again, his remarkable memory came to his aid. In order to get a license to sell real estate, a person was required to pass a state test. Daddy read through the material, passed the test with one of the highest scores, and in his first month of selling real estate, was named, "Salesman of the Month" with the highest sales in the area.

It didn't take long for him to realize that with his tremendous burden for souls, he had to make a choice between selling and ministering. He and mother talked it over. We were in school, so mother decided to go to work, and so free daddy to concentrate totally on the church.

What a lady my mother is! This story is about my father, but mother makes the story complete. She was behind him all the way, totally supporting him, encouraging him, loving him. She is an outstanding example of what a minister's wife can be. At that time, mother went to work in a hamburger drive-in as a cook, working for some people in the church. When she wasn't working on her job, she was helping daddy with all the clerical work, or helping with the Sunday school. She was also an excellent housekeeper. She had tremendous energy and a real zest for life. In the time it takes most people to make excuses about why they are too busy to do something, she would already have it done. She was always bursting into daddy's study with, "Oh, honey, do I ever have an idea!" He loved this in her, and encouraged her creativity. Things would really start to hum when mother would get an idea!

Daddy, as busy as he was in his pastorate, was not too busy to roll up his sleeves and help around the house. If mother was not yet home from work, he would start dinner. If a room got cluttered or needed vacuuming, he wouldn't step over the mess and wait until his wife got home, he would get out the vacuum and take care of it. What a beautiful example for us, watching our parents in action at home. They were the same at home as they were in public, and in the eyes of their congregation. There was no double standard in their behavior. Both of them cared for their church the same way. If something needed to be done, either one of them would take care of it. This remained true even when the congregation grew to 2,000 people. You could find daddy on Saturday night, with vacuum in hand, cleaning up something that had been missed, rather than getting on the phone and trying to find somebody else to do it.

11
STRENGTHEN THE THINGS THAT REMAIN

It was my senior year in high school. Charm was in junior high, Ted and Marilyn were both in grade school. Mother was working at the Bon Marche department store by this time and helping daddy in the office. There had been a steady growth in the church since moving to Latah Street. The unfinished balcony had now been finished, and was nearly filled. The Sunday school rooms were all bursting and the facilities were going to have to be expanded somehow. God's blessing was upon the congregation.

My parents went for a drive one day, when one of the tires went flat. Daddy couldn't get the jack to work, so with his great strength, he lifted up the little English Ford Anglia, and held it up while mother changed the tire. This wasn't the first time he had held up a light car but this time he didn't feel well afterwards. Several days later, he went to the doctor who told him to rest. He continued to grow weaker and finally went to a heart specialist. The specialist told him to report immediately to emergency. He had experienced a mild heart attack, but because he had waited, infection had set in and was raging through his body. By the time he got to the hospital, he was so weak that he could not even pick up his watch. He was out of his pulpit from the day after Easter until June.

One of the church board members, who had felt the call of God on his heart for the ministry but, up to that time, had not gone into full-time service, stepped forward and told mother and dad, "I believe God has placed me here for such a time as this!" Mother put her shoulder to the wheel, and with the help of that board member, Ed Jones, the congregation united, and together they worked and kept on going. Central Assembly did not even miss a step. In fact, during the time daddy was absent from the church, it continued to grow.

He had never in his life experienced any kind of nervous problem. He was the kind of person who, when he wanted to go to sleep, simply closed his eyes, and was asleep. But now, even the very gentle closing of a door would seem to go right through him. This strong giant of a man experienced such weakness that the day he could finally pick up his watch again was a real thrill. Once again, God was teaching him a lesson through trial. His capacity to understand people with nervous problems and people who were weak in body expanded. He was learning compassion for problems which before he might not have understood.

During the many weeks of recuperation, the Lord brought this phrase to his mind over and over again, "Strengthen the things that remain. Strengthen the things that remain!"

As daddy meditated on the meaning of the phrase the Lord had so burned on his heart, he began to search the scriptures and he discovered the Lord was talking about the things that would last for eternity. The Lord illuminated to his heart that those things which would remain were his relationship to God and family ties. He became even more aware of his own family, although he had always cherished every one of us. He had a new awareness of the things that really are important to God.

Years later, daddy shared with me that as the angel, Gabriel, was giving him these beautiful truths from God's Word, he reminded him of that time in the hospital when God spoke to him about the importance of the family.

Gabriel told my father that he was there as God continued to unfold His great plan in his life.

The keynote of all the messages brought by the angel from God was God's care and love for people, as evidenced by the sacrifice of Jesus. Over and over again, this message was given to daddy through divine messenger from many different portions of the Bible. He was reminded of how God portrayed His plan for the family in the Old Testament in Exodus 30:12-16, and Exodus 38:25-28. At that time, God wanted the name of every head of the house and his family included in the gate of the tabernacle. So, now, through the sacrifice of Jesus, He reserves a place for the whole family, but each member must individually be born again. The angel shared with daddy that if one person in the family was saved, the entire family was highly favored because of the prayers of this one individual. The angel said that he was now leading a host of angels to clear the way, to scatter the enemies, to move away the roadblocks, and to let people know that the heart of the Father is warm toward them!

After recovering from this heart attack, daddy returned to his pulpit, and was soon vigorously back to work for the kingdom. As a result of the way the Lord dealt with him during the time he was recuperating, his family counseling ministry began to expand. In his messages to his people, he began to stress the things that were really important to God, the things that would last for eternity.

When the church moved to its new location on Latah, daddy felt it would be good to have the family move closer to that area. The first house the Buck family moved into near the church was brand new, but it was very small. It had three bedrooms for a family of eight. Mother's parents had come to live with us for a while due to the illness of my grandfather. Daddy made the garage of the new house into a bedroom, but it was still very close quarters.

He came home one day brimming with excitement. He had found a fabulous deal on a house! It had four bedrooms, a full basement, with possibilities for a family room, a huge yard with lots of shade trees and a swimming pool! Talk about an excited family, especially the four of us children!

What a place for teenagers! The parsonage became the center of activity for all the young people, especially during the beautiful, hot, lazy days of summer.

The people in the church worked hard, but when it was time to play they had a good time.

Some of the people in the church were practical jokers, and at one of the Sunday school picnics they had a good one to try on my dad. He loved cream puffs, so someone baked the most beautiful batch and brought them to the picnic. One of those gorgeous cream puffs, however, was full of Tobasco sauce. This special treat was offered to daddy. Everything got really quiet except for a snicker here and there as he took a giant mouthful of cream puff. The eyes of the practical jokers got bigger and bigger, as he exclaimed how delicious it was, and without even blinking, finished it off and licked his finger. He had turned the practical joke on them.

The next day, however, he was really sick. But even in his misery, he told me he thought it was worth it to see the look on the faces of those people, as they waited, and waited, and waited.

12
THE ORB OF TRUTH

The years passed and there continued to be constant, steady growth in Central Assembly. The messages that daddy shared from his pulpit were messages of God's love and forgiveness.

People began to stream into his office for counseling. From the alcoholic to the person with nervous problems, God endued my father with divine wisdom in sharing the help that was available to them in Jesus Christ. Couples with marital problems began to find new hope for their marriages. The message concerning the things that are important to God that he had received during his illness was so burned into his heart that it was reflected in every part of his ministry.

Men and women from all walks of life began to worship regularly at Central Assembly. People dressed in expensive fur coats sat next to people from the wrong side of town, loving each other and the Lord. Visitors would walk into the church and exclaim at the presence of the Lord they could feel in that place and the essence of love filling the entire building.

Because of daddy's sensitivity to people, and God's touch on his life, he was able to ride out problems that could have caused a lot of hurt and division.

Not everyone understood the mesages that my father had to share. Some people thought he was preaching too much love, and not enough of God's judgment.

Finally the men on the church board were approached about having to vote of confidence taken at the next business meeting. One of the men on the board took daddy out to lunch. Then, out by the river in one of Boise's parks, he shared with him what the comments were. My father's heart was broken. All he had been sharing was the God that he knew. A God of love. A God who gave heaven's best, Jesus, so that a lost world could be reconciled to the Father. As the two men sat together in the quietness of Julia Davis Park on the bank of the Boise River, the sunlight glistened on the tears that streamed down my father's face. Those tears came from the depths of a loving heart.

The sweetness of Jesus radiated from dad as he called that crucial business meeting to order. He quietly led in prayer before the vote was to be taken. Suddenly the power of God flooded that business meeting. The board members had heard that there was going to be a landslide vote of "No Confidence," but to their amazement, when the votes were counted, the votes of confidence in daddy's ministry were overwhelming, with only three or four out of the whole membership against! Before the foundation of the world, God had a plan for my father's life, and nothing and no one could stop the unfolding of His divine purposes.

God confirmed daddy's ministry then, and again years later when God sent the following message to him through the angel, Gabriel.

Gabriel gave Dad a reference from God's Word to confirm the truths he taught (Jer. 9:23, 24). Here, in dad's own words is the message preached to the congregation on, "The Orb of Truth."

"God is stating that He wants the world to know Him as He is! He said, 'Let not the wise man glory in his wisdom neither let the mighty man glory in his might, let not the rich man glory in his riches: But let him that glorieth glory in this,

71

that he understandeth and knoweth me, as a God full of loving kindness, a God of mercy, a God of righteousness, a God of justice, in these things I delight saith the Lord.'

"One thing that God spoke to my heart in this connection is that the world as a whole has the truth about what God is like, but they have the truth upside down. God wants the world to know that He cares for them. The world of theology has had a picture of God. They've had the orb of truth that God is a God of compassion and He's a God of wrath, both sides, but God through an angel said, 'They have the order reversed. They have the gospel inverted.' Their message, to a large extent, is that we must see Him first of all as a God of wrath who must be appeased through various ways and efforts. If somehow you can appease the wrath of God by what you do, by what you're able to achieve or how you perform, you may drop through this area of His wrath, and enter into His love. Therefore, the message of His love has always been one that was bound and wrapped in a package of conditions. If we do, He will do. But the truth is, God's love is unconditional!

"When He spoke to Moses, you remember how Moses cried out, 'God let me see you, I want to see you as you really are.' God said, 'You can't see me.' But Moses said, 'I want to see you face to face, I want to talk with you.'

God said, 'I'll tell you what I'll do. I'll put you in this little cleft of the rock, and I'm going to put my big hand over the top, and then I'm going to pass by, and let you get a little feel of the glory, and then I'm going to give you a personal picture of how I want to be seen, what I'm really like.' So you read it in Exodus 34:6 and 7 where the Lord passed by, and He spoke to Moses out of the glory cloud, and He said, 'The Lord God, full of loving kindness, graciousness, full of compassion and mercy.' Then He went on so Moses would have the full picture, and He said, 'To those who refuse and reject, they'll know the wrath of God.' So this message today has turned the orb of truth over, and God is saying, 'Let men and women know that if they'll plunge into my love, and accept it, they need never experience my wrath!'

"But if they only know about wrath first, then they're seldom able to accept His love because there's always that fear. All this love is wonderful. But they are so conditioned to His wrath, it's difficult to enter into His love. God has ways of cleansing and causing those memories of the past to lose their power to hurt. He says, 'Go out and carry this message of My love.' The world is so anxious to hear this message that a week ago when my wife and I were out ministering, and it has been the same thing every place we've gone, the buildings were filled long before service time."

Daddy never chastised the people who had wanted to have him voted out, he just loved them. Soon they, too, responded to the beautiful nature of our heavenly Father as it streamed out from the life of His obedient servant.

God had given dad a glimpse of himself that he had to share with a world that was lost. People already knew they were condemned and lost. Daddy shared with them Jesus who could give them a new life. Many people found Christ, and my father continued to have reconciliation as his highest priority.

13
PLUGGED INTO GOD'S HEART

It was early the Saturday morning before Easter, 1966, when daddy woke up to unbelievable pain in his chest. He got up, thinking it would help him feel better, and collapsed to the floor. Mother called the ambulance.

My sister, Charm, was awakened by the dog barking in the garage. She got up to find daddy lying in the hall on a stretcher. She leaned over to kiss him, and he said weakly, "I don't feel very good." He was almost gone. The ambulance attendants shook their heads. They were sure he would not make it to the hospital.

My husband Alan and I received a call at home and our trip to the hospital is just a blur in my mind. I loved dad so much that I couldn't bear to think that anything could happen to him.

He was still alive, although just barely, when he arrived at emergency where he was immediately put into Intensive Care. He told me later that the pain was so intense, and the pressure on his chest so great, he almost could not bear it. He experienced this pressure and agonizing pain for six or seven hours.

At the parsonage, my brother Ted woke up to find that his beloved father was very ill. Mother had come back from the hospital to care for the children. She and Ted went into the bedroom, and together, they knelt by the bed, praying for husband and father.

In Intensive Care, daddy suddenly felt something begin to go through his body. It started at the top of his head and progressed slowly down to his toes. This sensation lasted about thirty minutes.

He said later that it was like walking from a room filled with pain through a doorway into another room totally free from pain. When he opened his eyes, he felt completely well. He took off the oxygen tubes and sat up. The nurse came running in. He told her, "I want to go home! I'm well!" He got out of bed and said, "Where are my clothes?" More nurses came running. They thought he was going to die and had just one last surge of strength. They tried to get him back into bed. But he told them, "I have to go, I have to preach at my Easter services tomorrow!" They frantically called the doctor and he told daddy that he absolutely could not be released until they had tested him thoroughly!

That day was spent in tests of all kinds but they could find absolutely nothing wrong with him.

The doctor made him stay overnight on Saturday, but Sunday morning, Ted went to pick him up to bring him to the Easter morning service. The congregation was thrilled as their pastor walked onto the platform. Many of them had heard that he was near death just the day before. There was a standing ovation and applause to the Lord.

Daddy told me later that while preaching his message on the Resurrection, he happened to glance down at his wrist. The hospital band was still there. It almost overwhelmed him as he realized that on this Easter he, too, had experienced the resurrection power of Christ in his own body.

School was out for Easter vacation so the next day the church had a picnic. We knew for sure that God had touched dad, because for several hours he played softball with all of the young people, and he didn't even feel the effects of the exertion.

14
FOUR LITTLE BUCKS
AND HOW THEY GREW

As a result of the angelic visitations to my father, the light of scrutiny was turned on our family. What kind of children did this man raise? The proof of his credibility in the eyes of many of his colleagues was how did those children turn out? Did he really practice what he preached?

I believe that all four of us are a testimony to our parents' ministry.

I was born dramatic. I walked and talked at seven months, much to my father's delight, and as described earlier, I started singing when I was very young. I was ill many times during my school years, even suffering a relapse of rheumatic fever every winter until I was fifteen years of age. At that time I outgrew this problem. Because of daddy's interest in me and his help with my school work, I was never held back, but was able to graduate with my class. I wanted to be just like my dad, and the highest compliment I could receive especially when I got particularly feisty, was when my mother would sigh, and say with a laugh, "Oh, Sharon, you're just like your father." I loved it, although I wasn't really. I was totally uncoordinated, dreamy, flirty, scatterbrained, but musically inclined. I did share, however, my father's deep love for people.

I loved to read, and although my pictures in those years deny it, daddy thought I was beautiful and that I could do anything I wanted to do. When I was younger and during times of better health, I would produce plays for the neighborhood for a penny a ticket. When I was ill, I would get all the neighborhood children to come in and keep me company by telling them fantastic stories. When I got older I was always bringing home stray, hurting people I would find, saying, "You come home and meet my daddy. He'll help you!"

When I got a little older, I would overhear my dad saying half proudly and half despairingly to his friends, "I have to beat off the boys with a baseball bat!" Of course, I just ate that up! I loved my father so much, I would rather have died than do anything to hurt him. And because of his guidance and low pressure on his highstrung and dreamy daughter, he helped me develop a glowing trust in the God he served.

Charm was fun. She was a born tomboy, and an athlete with a mathematical mind like her father. I liked to dress nicely and keep my hair just so even as a very little girl and used to despair of my little sister, who up through age nine, loved to put her hair up on those little pink rubber curlers first thing in the morning, and leave them in. As the day passed, more and more hair would come out of those curlers, but Charm was too busy to care. She would button her own dress in the back, missing one of the buttons and be ready for the day. She didn't want to take time to wash her face, and would do so only with the greatest urging. Her favorite spot to meditate was the very top of the street sign on the corner by the parsonage. She would shinny up the sign and perch there like a vulture, watching the cars go by. It was funny to watch passersby do a double take, as they saw a little girl with pink rubber curlers, from which the hair was sticking out like a fan around her head, sitting very calmly on top of the street sign, watching them drive by. This delightful little character, so opposite from her older sister, was a tremendous balance for me. She grew up to be a lovely sparkly woman and totally feminine. Charm and I enjoy a very special, fun relationship as sisters today.

Ted came into the world hungry and big. One of the family's fondest memories of Ted was seeing him spread thick peanut butter on half a dozen pieces of bread, and with them carefully lined up both long arms, he would gingerly balance his "bedtime snack" as he went downstairs to his bedroom, calling good night to everybody.

He grew tall and skinny, and the fact that his ears stuck out was accentuated by the crewcut he always wore, because it would last, and haircuts were expensive. Unfortunately he had a terrible temper when he was younger, but again, because of the love and guidance of our father, he learned to control it. He was a loving, sensitive little boy, and had an unusual relationship with the Lord from a very early age. He was a natural scholar, and loved to read almost to the exclusion of other activities. Daddy's loving guidance got him out of his books and into sports. He eventually was honored after an exciting high-school and college career in football, to try out for the Dallas Cowboys, a top-rated professional football team. He was cut during training, but it was very special to all of us in the family that he had the opportunity to try out. We knew that his athletic ability had developed through the influence of a father who chose to spend time with his son.

Marilyn, or Mimi as we called her, was a delight to her father as well as to us older sisters, and she really kept Ted's life from being boring. She was two years younger than he, and a real go-getter. Daddy's nickname for her was "Gravel Gertie", because she had such a hoarse, gravelly little voice. She grew up to be a lyric soprano, with a keen ear for music. She had beautiful thick blonde hair, the envy of both of her sisters, who loved to comb and fix it. She had the most unusual light blue eyes, fringed by black eyelashes. She was stubborn, and when she was spanked by mother, she would only laugh. Her sense of humor was outstanding, and she could make daddy laugh more than any of the rest of us.

She had a terrible time sleeping, and many times in the middle of the night Charm and I would wake up to find Mimi standing in the doorway of our bedroom, just staring, willing us to wake up so she could ask to crawl in bed with one of us. We finally took pity on our little sister, who being the youngest, didn't enjoy the fellowship we had, and bought three trundlebeds, and asked Mimi to move into our bedroom. She was delighted. We would try to wait until she was asleep before exchanging secrets, finding out later that she heard every word we said.

It is a real lesson in psychology to read from each Buck offspring how we felt about our father, and his handling of each of us as we grew up.

Since I'm the oldest, I get to start!

SHARON: "One of the first things I remember about my father was his generosity. He was the kind of man who gave everything he had to the Lord, to his family, and to people in need. I remember when a tramp knocked on our door when I was about four years old. It was during the time that I had rheumatic fever. I remember my dad going to the door, and there was a grizzled, shabby, little old man. Dad let him in and fixed him a bowl of soup. Then he had him chop some wood for him, in order to earn some money. I was so impressed with how he treated this old man, even leaving him his dignity, that I asked my daddy to bring in my piggy bank, which had about one-hundred pennies in it. I remember wanting to be just like my dad, and I asked him to give the old man my pennies. He gave me a big smile, and asked, 'Are you sure you want to do this, honey?' I assured him that I did.

"He used to include the whole family in his ministry. I remember the fun days when we first moved to Boise, and our church was small. Our whole family would get together and help fold, address, and put out the weekly newsletter after daddy typed it up. He had taught himself to type, and he typed as fast with two or three fingers as a lot of people could using five fingers on each hand. We would laugh and talk and just have a great time.

"Daddy always got a big kick out of the fact that I was so dramatic, but this trait could have tried a lesser man's patience. Charm always thought, until she was older, that I got spanked much harder than she did, because from the first moment I found I was going to be spanked, until long afterwards, I would howl at the top of my voice and really put on a show. I can remember sitting on my bed across from Charm, with my legs straight out in front of me, my back against the wall, my head thrown back, really carrying on. I remember Charm, after her spanking, (we usually got one together), crying a few tears, and then with her eyes as big as saucers, watching her poor big sister.

"Whenever daddy punished us, it was never in anger. After the spanking was over, or in later life whatever punishment had been meted out, he would come to us and say, 'Honey, I just hate punishing you, but I'm responsible to God for your life. You still love your old dad though, don't you?' What do you do with a dad like that? I would always have to say, 'Sure I do, daddy!' Later on, when he would have to deny us something, or an activity, for our own good, and I would be pouting, he just couldn't stand it! I always knew it wouldn't be long before I would hear his footsteps outside my door, and then he would come in. He never would change his mind, but he'd say, 'You forgive your old dad for being such an old meanie, don't you?' I would always have to say yes, and most of the time I would have to tell him he was right about whatever it was he wouldn't let me do. A lot of times I would go to him even before he would come to me and tell him, 'You were right, daddy' because I never could stand to think that he felt badly. What a dad! It really makes me lonesome thinking about what a lucky girl I was to have a dad like that. With my inborn nature, I could have been so different.

"His patience with all of us was also a beautiful trait. Now that I have children, I try to be very careful not to laugh at some of the things that matter to them. His patience and care were very vividly illustrated when I was about eleven. I came home in heart-rending tears. A little boy in the sixth grade I really liked was moving away. I would never see him again! I cried and cried. My daddy comforted me the best way he could. Then I got an idea. 'Daddy, would you take me in the car, by his house, for just one last look at him?' Daddy didn't laugh, he just said, 'Sure, honey.' So off we went for one last glimpse of that boy and his house. Daddy did get in one of his famous stories, however! He told me that he had a friend who had fallen in love, and the girl decided to marry someone else. He told me very dramatically how that friend just sat by the window and pined away, getting skinnier and skinnier, and weaker and weaker, because he couldn't get over his lost love! The story was so dramatic he finally made me giggle, and I told him, 'Oh, daddy, I would never do that!'

"A beautiful memory of my daddy's care and generosity occurred when I was fourteen. I was going to have my very first date to a special banquet. We didn't have any money, and although I really would have liked a new dress, I realized it was impossible. My best dress was a hand-me-down from a wealthy friend. I had worn it many times, but it was still nice. I felt badly about not having a new dress for such a special occasion but tried very hard to hide my feelings because I knew there was no money for any extras at that time. I told my daddy that it was all right for me to wear the dress I already had, and gave him a big hug.

"The big day finally came. I came home from school all excited about my first date. When I walked in the door, my mother gave me a cute little smile and said, 'Run upstairs, honey. There's something on your bed!' I tore up to my bedroom, and there lying on my bed was the most beautiful dress I had ever seen. It was navy blue with white stripes and very full and swirly. It had a navy blue cummerbund to emphasize my waist. It was the latest style. It was gorgeous!

Mother told me later that Daddy somehow got the extra

money, probably by going without something himself, and had gone downtown, to pick out that beautiful dress. He had gone out of his way to make my first date very special.

"My dad always went with me to youth camp, because he was in great demand as a teacher for young people. I didn't really mind, although he did keep an eye on me as far as the fellows were concerned. I was proud of him, because he was always the pitcher for the softball team when the kids played against the preachers, and I felt that because of his pitching, the preachers always won!

"I remember one year my dad called me aside the last night of camp. He was very excited. The kids had voted on camp king and queen and I had been voted the youth camp queen! It was supposed to be a surprise, and the winners were to be announced at the banquet that night, but dad just couldn't wait to see my face as he told me himself! He was tickled, just as much as I was.

"On the last night, after the banquet, everyone wanted to do something memorable, and my friends and I were no exception. We had been gathering clothes from the counsel-ors' wash all week, with plans to build a funny dummy counselor the last night, and put it in the main recreation area. I shared this with my dad, because he always got such a big kick out of the harmless pranks we did. This night, however, he told me that he had heard some of the kids were planning to get in real trouble by sneaking out of camp and going to town for the whole night. He asked me if I would give up my plans and stay in my tent that night after curfew, so nobody could point any fingers at me. I reluctant-ly promised him I would, and he said, 'Okay, honey, I know you've promised me, so I can count on you!' I couldn't break a promise to my dad, so after the exciting banquet, and having a wonderful time as queen, I went to my cabin with my friends and my counselor and went to sleep.

"The next morning, everybody was buzzing about the kids who had stayed out all night, and for some reason, the counselors thought I was one of them. My counselor told them that I had stayed in all night, and they told her she was lying for me! They went to my dad, and told him he would have to talk to his daughter for going out all night, 'and *her*, queen of camp, just the night before!'

"My dad just looked them right in the *eye*, and said, 'I don't have to talk to her. She promised me she wouldn't leave her cabin, and I believe she kept her promise! If she said she stayed in, she did!'

"When I heard my dad say that, my heart stirred with a strong determination to always be worthy of the trust that he placed in me. He never did even ask me privately, 'Did you, or did you not stay in?' As far as he was concerned, the issue was closed. I didn't really care then what the other people thought, because my dad believed me!

"Daddy really used his diplomatic ability in one incident when I was in high school. He had an ironclad rule that I could not go steady. During the late fifties and early sixties it was popular to wear a big class ring from your boyfriend, wrapped up in string covered with fingernail polish. My friends were all going steady, and I wanted to also.

"One night, I accepted a class ring from one of my boyfriends. I had it all figured out how I was going to change my dad's mind about going steady. I would go to all the work of wrapping yards of string around this ring, polish it with nail polish, then tell my dad that I didn't care about going steady, but that I had gone to all that work, and what I really wanted was a big ring like all my friends. He didn't need to worry about me liking the boy too much.

Daddy listened with great interest as I showed him my handiwork, and told him how very long it had taken me to get the ring fixed up. He smiled when I continued my little spiel about how I actually didn't care at all about going steady, but that all I wanted was a big ring like all my friends. He gave me a bear hug and said, 'Why, honey, is that all you wanted?' I nodded, crossing my fingers. Maybe he *was* going to let me keep my ring! He continued, 'If I had know that's all you wanted, we could have taken care of it a long time ago.

Tell you what, you give that ring back, and I'll buy you the biggest ring you have ever seen, bigger than that one, and you can wrap it to your heart's content!'

"I know a lot of preachers' kids who hated it because their fathers were always telling them they had to be an example for the people in their church. As a result, they didn't feel like they could ever be themselves. I always felt my dad was special because he encouraged us to be ourselves, and develop in our own way. He didn't even punish us all the same way or have all our rules alike. He treated each one of us individually, and made decisions about our actions based on the merit of each case that came up. Because of this, each of us felt that we held our own very special place in his attention. He felt that each one of his children could do anything they tried, and was a great encourager, never once tearing us down but always building up our self-esteem. He asked us to share with him in his ministry, saying that we could help him by developing the trust of his congregation in his ministry by the way we responded. We all took this very seriously, feeling as if we were working arm-in-arm with him on almost the same level of responsibility.

"When I met my husband-to-be under very unusual circumstances, my dad was very concerned because he didn't know anything about Alan or his background. He called Alan's pastor and also his parents to find out what kind of person he was. I remember sitting in the front yard with dad, feeling a little resentful. I was twenty years old and I felt I knew what I was doing. Instead of responding to my resentment with anger, he said, 'Honey, when God gave you to me, it was as if He entrusted me with a precious treasure. To me you are like a beautiful, priceless pearl necklace. I just can't leave my beautiful treasure lying around carelessly for anyone to pick up!' His voice broke and as I looked at him I saw tears running down his cheeks.

All I could do was put my arms around his neck and cry with him. I thanked him, and later I thanked God for giving me a daddy who cared so very much about me.

Later on I had to chuckle over another little episode with dad about Alan. Alan had to be away in the service for about six months. He considered us unofficially engaged, but I didn't, so I continued happily dating a lot of different young men. Finally one day, my dad said in a very official voice, 'Sharon, would you please come to my office!' I racked my brain trying to remember whether I had done anything wrong lately. I couldn't think of anything. He sat me down and got right to the point. He asked me if Alan knew I was dating while he was away. Sheepishly I said No. Then my dear daddy told me I had three alternatives. I could keep on dating, but I was to let Alan know; or if I couldn't tell Alan, he would; or I could stop dating, and the case would be closed. I decided to quit dating.

Then daddy told me how he felt Alan had special qualities that would complement me, and that he would be happy if Alan should be his son-in-law someday.

One last thing that made me happy was that when dad experienced the visitations of the angels, he was allowed to go with them on several occasions to visit heaven. He knew what a joyful person I was, and he told me that I would be very excited to know that the atmosphere of heaven was joy and happiness. He said that while he was allowed to be there, he could hear the angels laughing. The one thing that was obviously lacking was solemnity and piety. He knew I would be thrilled with this as would be a lot of other people. He encouraged people to laugh more and be happy here, because, he would tease them, they would surely be out of place in heaven if they lived their Christianity with long faces and a lack of joy.

CHARM: "I remember, with great affection, dad's relationship with me as his tomboy. Until Ted was old enough to be in sports, and really get out and do things, I was my dad's little tomboy, and still have a streak that runs a mile wide. I remember dad always being on the sidelines of the track meets and softball games. I could always be assured that although he couldn't always be there for the whole thing, he would show up and was interested in what I was doing, and in the things that were going on in my life. I remember his pride when I would win in a track meet or when I got on the all-city softball team for the summer. As I got older and wasn't really involved in those things, when a boy would come over to the house for dinner, dad would always push back his chair at the end of the meal and while we were talking about different things, he would insist that I go get my ribbons! I had no real interest in showing a boy my ribbons, and they probably didn't want to see them either, but to dad, it was a real point of pride. As I see my kids growing up, I can understand why he felt the way he did, because any accomplishment of theirs is a big highlight in my life.

"I really appreciated him making a big thing out of the good little things, never making a big thing out of the bad, and giving us real self-esteem. We never had any question as to how big we were in the eyes of our mom and dad. They always went as far as they could in trusting us and lifting and building us up.

"I remember dad taking all of us out on the back roads of Boise and teaching us how to drive long before we were old enough, and his tremendous patience. He used to take Sharon out, and I would always tag along. I would listen very carefully, then when we would get back and Sharon and dad would go in the house, I would stay in the car and practice shifting. When it was my turn to learn, dad was surprised at how much I already knew, because I had been practicing on the side.

"I remember so well when I was fourteen. I had just received my license and dad had bought one of the first new cars we had ever had. It was a 1960 Ford, considered a real dog today, but it was exciting then because it was brand new off the lot.

"On a Sunday afternoon, I asked dad if I could take a bunch of girls and go out to dinner. His response, was, 'Sure, honey, no problem.' So I took our brand new car, and away we went with a carload of fourteen-year-old girls, none of whom had their licenses. Naturally, I was a big celebrity.

"I turned a corner too sharply where there was a curb that stuck up about two feet. As we drove over it, there was a crunching sound. It sounded horrible! I thought for sure we had ruined the whole car. I pulled over, and the car door wouldn't open. I was absolutely shattered. Going home, of course I was worried about what dad's response would be. I went in and told him what had happened. He got up very calmly and said, 'Let's go take a look at it!' He looked and felt underneath the car. The door was jammed and wouldn't open. Then he said, 'Well, I guess we're going to have to get it fixed!' I was ready to lay my life on the line, and to have him attach my salary from the drive-in where I worked to pay for it. His response has been a help to me through the early years of my children's lives, because when I overreact to a situation, I think of dad and his response to something that many fathers would have reacted to so differently. Dad knew that I had already punished myself so completely that he wasn't going to add to it.

"One thing he's told us as parents, and I think of it so often, is to never make the punishment greater than the crime. He had a basic, solid, consistent approach to us as children, we always knew where he stood.

"I remember him as being a very strong disciplinarian. In early years, dad's word was final. When his voice got a certain tone in it, then we didn't ask any more questions. We were all familiar with the trips to the basement and dad's big belt. But spankings were always given with kindness and love, and we never questioned how he felt about us.

"When we got older, the discipline changed to giving us as much rope as we could handle. With each individual it was different, because we were all put together differently. If he saw, however, that we were making a wrong decision, he always kept the last word in his hip pocket. He loved us enough, when this happened, to put his reputation and his relationship with us on the line, and take a stand that many times was hard, but with his guidance turn us back in the right direction. I feel this is the reason why we are all serving the Lord today; because he had the strength of character to risk being unpopular with his children, and take a stand that would assure us our future happiness. He did this with all of us, giving us leeway, and teaching us how to make our own decisions, but keeping us pointed in the right direction.

"Speaking of this, I was twenty years old and had been a bridesmaid for a friend. I had entertained one of her grooms-men, who had come from out of town and wasn't a Christian. Dad had not felt good about him at the time, and then I had stayed out later than I should have. Dad was rather disappointed in me. The next time the young man came to town, he called and wanted to go out with me. Being a tender-hearted person and not wanting to hurt his feelings, even though I wasn't particularly interested, I left him on the phone and asked dad what he thought. He very definitely told me what he thought, 'No! I don't want you to go out with him, I didn't get good vibrations from him!' I said, 'But dad, he's on the telephone, and I don't know what to tell him.' Dad said, 'If you can't tell him no, then I will.' So dad picked up the phone and said, 'I'm sorry, but my daughter can't go out with you!'

"I could have felt a little rebellious thinking that dad had overstepped his bounds. But looking back I realize he loved me enough to jeopardize his popularity in a sense, and make a decision that he knew was for my good. I hope that as my kids grow older, I'll have the strength to do that with them.

"Dad had a pet name for me. He called me 'Chump' or affectionately, 'Charmi'. Being dad's boy, he used to take his Chump with him to minor league baseball games. I would hang on every word as he told me about the different players on the Boise Braves club. I wanted to make dad feel good about being there with me. I was interested, but probably not as interested as I acted. I loved the privilege of going someplace with dad by myself. Ted and Marilyn were too young, Sharon was probably on a date, and mom thought it was nice that we could go together. So we would go and have a hot dog, and watch the game.

Something else I really enjoyed as dad's 'boy', was going fishing with him. Neither one of us was much of a fisherman and we would usually end up where all the flies were. Some of the times I have mentioned did not happen too often but they were very special times and quality times that make for good memories.

"Something else that dad used to do for me was make up all kinds of mathematical story problems for me to figure out. That's how we made the time pass when we were on vacations and had to spend a lot of time driving.

"Spiritually, dad gave us a legacy for which there is no substitute. It has made our lives richer than any kind of inheritance. We saw in his life a stability, a steadfastness, a solid interpretation of the Scripture, and a real understanding of the nature of God.

"Dad talked a lot about what God was like. If someone would ask a specific question, dad could answer it, not only on the basis of the Scripture, but on the basis of actually knowing what God was like. I feel like everyone associated with dad got a glimpse into the personality of God, because dad knew His personality so well that he even radiated it.

"I don't think that there was any one of us who ever wanted to do anything but live for God. There may have been times of rebellion to parental control, but none of us went through a period where we didn't want to serve God. I don't think there was any question in our minds or in mom's and dad's minds as to whether we would serve God, because He was such a part of our lives.

"I always appreciated dad's approach to the ministry, and to our family. He never used the old adage that we had to do such and such because he was a preacher. He would say, "You're my child and this is how I feel. You do this because it's what I want you to do." If the decision was unpopular with the congregation, that wasn't an issue. He made his decisions based on his own personal feelings of how he wanted us to grow up, not how the congregation wanted us to grow up.

"I can never forget the first time Bryan, my husband, came into the life of our family. I had come home from Northwest College at Christmas time, knowing that I was going to have to break up with a young man who had been important to me for a long time. My first night home, I told the young man that I had met someone who was going to become part of my life. I went home and proceeded to cry all night.

"The next morning I looked like a real hag. I finally got enough composure to put on some makeup and go to breakfast. No sooner had I sat down when dad came in and said, 'Well, so and so has sure grown up to be a fine young man, Charmi!' I ran from the table in tears, leaving poor dad standing there with a 'what did I do?' look on his face! Bryan arrived a few days later and proposed to me on the way back to college. Dad had had very little time with him, because we were so busy with all the Christmas activities and parties while we were home, so we decided that we would wait several weeks before calling him. Bryan finally called dad and asked for my hand in marriage. Dad's teasing response was, 'You don't want *her,* she'll just be a chain around your neck!' This really took Bryan by surprise. I asked dad in later years how he had felt about saying yes to a young man he had barely met. He told me, "Charmi, I had enough faith and confidence in you to know that if you loved him, it was right!" It really gave me a warm feeling to know that he trusted me to that point.

"Another quality that was outstanding in dad was his generosity. If he had one dollar in his pocket or in the bank and we needed a dollar, he would clean out his wallet for us, which was sometimes disturbing to mother. On special days for mom, he always wanted to give her a big surprise. I'll never forget when he had the living room and dining room recarpeted as a surprise for her. I don't think she was ever really crazy about the carpet, but dad never knew it. He was so proud and happy to have done something special.

"A special memory to me, especially now that dad is gone, is something that dad gave me. Mom and I went shopping in early fall for a new winter coat which I needed very badly. I had been married for several years, and my husband was also in the ministry. I picked one out and put it on layaway, thinking that it would probably take me to the end of the next year to pay for it. Just a few days before Christmas, mom and dad came knocking at my door. Dad was hiding something behind his back. With a "Merry Christmas" and a big hug, they presented me with my coat. I don't think I'll ever let that coat wear out!

"When dad laughed, he would throw his head back and his whole body would laugh. One such time was when a lady had come up to the front of the church to give her testimony. She began to get really inspired and her throat got a little dry. There was a little cup there that looked like it was filled with water, but it was anointing oil. This lady took a big swallow of that oil, and dad literally exploded on the platform. He could hardly sit on his chair. Of course the whole congregation joined in, because when dad laughed, everyone around him laughed too. It was great to make dad happy; his big smile would light up his whole face.

"Dad always concealed his hurts. I know there were a lot of times through the years when he was hurting for one reason or another, but he never let this affect the temperament of our home. As a result, our home was very stable and peaceful.

"In later years when he received criticism in relationship to his experiences with the angels, he was hurt more than he would let anybody know. He didn't like being on the firing line, but because of his strong character, he would prefer to turn the other cheek, and express only love and concern for those who maligned him. He always maintained his positive ministry of how God loved us and how many miles God was willing to go with us, and how very much God was willing to forgive people."

TED: "Dad was always my very best friend. At the age of two, he was my best friend, at the age of ten, twelve, and all through the adolescent years, which would normally be a time of rebellion, dad was my best friend. I could bring anything to him. He would never put me down, and always made me feel special. Had it not been for the fact that he performed my marriage ceremony, he would have been the best man at my wedding.

"Dad showed all of us what God is like, not only by what he said, but how he lived. He was closer to God than any man I have ever known. He was the most consistent man I have ever known. I never received punishment from him in anger. I never heard him yell at any of us kids or at mom, and I never heard him and mom argue in front of us. I'm sure they must have had disagreements, but he showed us the nature of Christ. He was also the most generous and giving person I've met.

"One of the things that really stands out in my mind about my dad was his interest in the sports in which I was involved. Even as a youngster I was too tall for my coordination. I had just as much as everybody else, but it was spread out a lot thinner. When I started playing football in the fourth grade, dad was always there. He would come to as many practices as he could, even though he was very busy. He was always at the game unless he was sick. I could count on it. He would come and stand through an entire game, just so he could watch me get in for the last thirty seconds or one minute.

"One year we got back late from our vacation and football had already started. I was so tall and skinny I had to play with kids a year older because of my size. When I went out to practice, they had already been practicing for one or two weeks. It was rough on me that day, because they were in shape and I wasn't. At the end of that practice I told dad, 'I think I'm going to have to quit, I just can't do this!' Dad didn't push me, but he told me something I'll never forget. 'You're tired right now. Don't make a decision when you're down!

Let's go home, get some supper, and get you cleaned up, then you can make up your mind.'

"Of course, after supper and getting cleaned up, I felt better. This was when I was in the sixth grade. I went on to finish that year, and as a result I played all through junior high and high school. I was able to earn a scholarship, and had four years of college paid for because of playing football. This happened because dad gave me the wisdom, and the guidance not to make a decision when I was down.

"Another thing that helped shape my life were two words that my father told me he wanted me to totally eliminate from my vocabulary. The two words, 'if only.' Those two words are so destructive and harmful to people. He told me to replace those words with 'next time.'

"Dad taught me from the time I was very young how to treat girls and women, partly from his own example of how he treated my mom and my sisters, with love and consideration. There's a strong bond between me and my sisters. One time, however, all dad's girls really got to him, and to me. I was eight or nine years old and haircuts were expensive, so dad decided to become my barber. He came home one night with a hair-cutting kit, and began to cut my hair. Dad was always so good at doing anything, that he had perfect confidence in his ability to cut my hair. But as he worked, he began to realize that it was going to take some practice in being able to get both sides the same, even on a crewcut. In getting the hair even, he kept cutting it shorter, and shorter. He was about half-way done when mom called everybody to supper.

When I sat down in my chair, my sisters and my mom just dissolved into laughter. They also were having fun, at dad's expense, teasing him about his barbering. I felt so bad that I left the table, got a towel and wrapped it around my head like a turban, thinking that would cause the girls to quit teasing. But when I came back to the table with my towel around my head, they exploded again. Finally, dad said in a very stern voice, 'The next one who laughs has to leave the table!' That was too much for my mother. She tried to stop herself, but burst into giggles. Dad was really nonplussed, and he looked at her and said, 'That means you too, Charm!' That did it. Mom ran from the table consumed with laughter. Giggles continued to break out throughout the entire meal, but afterwards dad finished my haircut. It was short all right, but with practice, he really did get pretty good at crewcuts.

"I remember a time when I was about eleven or twelve. I was worried because I didn't feel that I could totally surrender my life to God. I remember in our house on Federal Way, sitting at the bottom of the stairs looking up to the top of the stairs at my dad, and telling him, 'Dad, you know I want to serve God. I want to be used of Him, and I want Him to be able to do with me what He wants. I think I could be a minister, but dad, if God wants me to be a missionary, I just don't think I can do it!'

"In my own mind I didn't want to go some place and live in a grass hut, eat fishheads, be with a bunch of people I didn't know, and away from the ones I loved. He told me something that gave me such a trust in God. I have been able to pass this on to others, and it is this 'God will never call you to something without giving you such a strong desire to do it, that it will be the only thing you'll be happy doing.' At that point, I said, 'I guess that's right. That's the kind of God we serve, isn't it?' From that point on, I totally surrendered, and said, 'Okay, God, whatever you have, here I am.' All of us kids had one thing imparted to us, the fact that we could trust God, because He always had good things in store for us.

"When I was two years old, dad taught me to read by making some flash cards of the alphabet. He also taught me the name of every car and truck on the road, so that even at night, if we were out camping near a highway, I could tell the difference between the kinds of trucks just by listening to the motors, especially the diesels. I'm sure it was real wisdom on my dad's part, because he kept me so busy naming cars, I didn't have time to fuss when we were out on the road.

"Knowing how to read came in handy one time when I was about two years old. We had a dog, actually it was the neighbor's dog, but it adopted us, so the neighbors gave her to us because she was at our house all the time anyway. She was a big beautiful Chesapeake Retriever named Skeeter. I had heard about a little car called the King Midget, which was smaller than most cars. Because I was so fascinated by cars, Skeeter and I took off one day, without asking anybody, to find the King Midget. I got on my tricycle and we went all the way downtown. A policeman came along and saw I wasn't with an adult, so he brought me to the address on Skeeter's collar. When I got out of the car, everybody asked me if I was okay, and I said, 'Yup. Whenever I came to a sign that said, s-t-o-p, I stopped!'

"Dad also taught me how to memorize whole chapters in the Bible. He helped me with math. He had a way of always helping you solve your own problems. I would come to him with problems in second-level algebra or geometry or calculus, and I would say, 'I'm having a hard time with this problem, could you help me a little bit?' He'd say, 'Explain it to me,' and I would go through the problem and explain it all, and he would say, 'Where are you stumped?' I would explain that to him, and all of a sudden I would say, 'Wait a second, I see!' I would go ahead and figure out the problem, and then say, 'Thanks, dad, for helping me!' He provided a sounding board for me and when I had problems, I could talk with him and rather than always just hastily moving in and solving them or saying, 'Hey, I can't help you,' he allowed me to be able to see things through.

I remember one time when I was about four years old. Dad and I were walking downtown to the Post Office, and he couldn't figure out why I kept dropping back behind him. Finally he said, "Ted, why don't you come up here with me?" I told him, 'Well, daddy, you look so nice with your suit on, and these are my play jeans that I have on and they've got some patches on the knees, and I'm not really cleaned up. I'll walk behind you, because I don't want people to think that you're with me, because you look so good, and I look so bad!' Of course my dad just scooped me up in his arms and said, 'Son, it doesn't matter how you look. I'm always proud to be seen with you.'

"He was proud of all of us. He and mom made our home a sanctuary. We could always feel comfortable at home. I had a shoe size that kept up with my age—from age ten until finally my feet stopped growing at age and size fifteen. I had large ears, and I looked something like an "L" with radar mounted on top, walking down the halls at school. I would receive criticism from my peers because my feet were bigger than theirs, or my ears were bigger, or my coordination hadn't come into full bloom. Yet, when I went home, I always felt important. My opinion was important. I was special, because my folks made all of us feel that way. This has made me want to treat everybody the same way.

"Dad didn't just teach us rules, but principles and values to live by. We couldn't help but love God, because of the God we saw in our father's life. Church was a fun place to go because dad was there. We never had to be forced to go, because he made church so exciting. Dad made all of life exciting and fun. He was always the best athlete on the team, and was just plain fun to be around.

Dad would have been a fantastic athlete. He taught me how to swim, how to ride a full-size bike when I was five. He taught me how to drive, starting at age two. I used to sit on his lap and steer, then at ages six and seven, dad went to several conferences in Montana and I helped him drive. I had to sit on a pillow, but I was tall for my age. He would sit on the other side of the car, relaxing as I was driving, seemingly with total confidence in me.

"He expressed that beautiful confidence in me when I was still in high school. He had just bought a new Datsun 240Z that didn't even have a thousand miles on it. A friend and I were invited to speak at a retreat, and I was planning to drive my car, which was okay, but nothing flashy. It was snowing and we were going up to a ski retreat where there was a lot more snow. Dad tossed me the keys to that neat little sports car and said, 'Here Ted, take this. I think you'll have a good time in it, and it'll run really good on the trip!'

"Something funny happened on one of our vacations. We went to Yellowstone Park in an old Nash whose seats folded down to make a bed. The four kids slept in that car, and mom and dad slept in sleeping bags by the fire near the car. The fire was kind of dim, and something woke dad up. He noticed that there was a bear coming over to where he and mom were. He lay real still, and the bear almost stepped on his face. Then the bear began to rummage through some things, and dad tried very quietly to get mom's attention. He didn't want to scare her though, so he said very softly, 'Charm, there's a bear over there!' It took my mom about two seconds to get in the car, with dad close behind. He decided that the bear was going to take everything if he didn't do something, so he took a pair of old wingtip shoes and clapped the heels together. The noise scared the bear so much it ran and hid under an old-fashioned camp trailer, where it started scratching itself. It was so funny to see that old trailer going up and down, up and down as the bear scratched. Needless to say, six people slept in that little Nash that night.

"When I was a senior in high school, I finally got a consistent starting position in football. I had to work very hard, and dad really helped me because he was willing to go down to the park with me and time me in my starts. As I would run, he was continually encouraging me.

"Our team that year was one of the top ranked in the nation. When it was time for the starting game of the new season, and I ran out on the field to be introduced, I felt good, knowing that mom and dad were up there in the stands, and they were taking a little pride in me, especially after all dad's work with me. It was a greater feeling to know how they felt than even how I felt for myself. When I moved on to college football and ran out on the field for the first game my sophomore year, my thrill was in knowing that my mom and dad were in the stands, and I had made them proud as they continually encouraged me through many years of hard work.

"The one individual person on earth who has had more impact on my life than anyone else ever will have was my father. He put his stamp on me so deeply that I couldn't lose it even if I wanted to. I have met the man who most reminded me of God, and I'm sure I'll never meet anyone like him until the time when we go to be with the Lord.

"Dad had a trust in me, and as a result I did my best to live up to his expectations. One reason why I didn't smoke or take a drink of booze, or hot rod his cars or even my own car, was because I didn't want to disappoint him and mom. One of the worst things I could ever think about would be if I ever made my dad disappointed in me. I determined with God's help I was never going to bring dishonor to his ministry.

"Now that I am a pastor, people ask me what kind of a pastor I want to be. All they have to do is study Roland Buck as a pastor of a church, and they can see in him my model. He was not a perfect man, but he came as close as anybody I've ever known.

"Shortly before he died, I was with him and suddenly I felt overcome with love for him. I told him how much I loved him and appreciated him. I told him how much he and mom had helped me when I needed it, and given to me, even financially. He said, "We never had that much money we could give you," and I informed him that he had given me a legacy worth more than any amount of money he could ever have given me."

MARILYN—(MIMI): "One of the first things I remember about my dad was his great big smile. He used to sing a song called 'You can Smile!' On the last chorus you were supposed to leave off the word 'smile' and instead show as big a grin as you could, and then hum. Whenever dad would lead that song, everyone would burst into laughter because his smile was definitely ear-to-ear.

"He loved athletics and was so proud of mom as well as Ted, Charm and I because we all were very coordinated. I remember when I was little how he would talk about the home runs my mother could hit. He went to Charm and Ted's games, and finally it was my turn. He was so proud of my baseball prowess.

"I played on a softball team for several years. I loved to look over at the sidelines and see my father cheering me on. I would want to give more than 100 percent so he would be proud of me.

"He was a terrific baseball player himself. Our whole family used to go out into the back yard, and play baseball together. At church picnics, when the men played baseball, as dad got up to bat everyone in the outfield would back up. Boy, could he hit home runs.

"I remember one summer when I was about two we went swimming. Dad was teaching the other kids to swim, but since I was so young he didn't think I was listening. All of a sudden there was a splash as I jumped in to swim with the other kids. Dad told me later that as he looked around, all he could see floating on top of the water was long blonde hair. He quickly rescued me, expecting the worst. But as he pulled me out of the water, I said, 'I did what you told the other kids to do, daddy. I didn't breathe in the water!'

"Dad always showed he had confidence in his children. This confidence was keenly illustrated one time when we went on vacation to Washington. I had just gotten my driver's license before we were to take our vacation and I wanted the chance to do some driving. I asked my dad if I could drive and he told me that, if I really wanted to drive, I would have to drive the stretch of the Ellensburg Canyon. At that time, there was only a two-lane road with a steep drop-off to a river on one side and the mountain on the other, plus it was very curvy. The thought of driving that stretch of road scared me, but I knew if I wanted to drive, I would have to overcome my fear. I took over the wheel with a lump in my throat. I think my mother, who was riding in the back seat, had an even bigger lump in her throat. I started down the steep, curvy road and began to relax. Dad would help me by telling me when I should brake for a corner and would encourage me and tell me I was doing fine. This is just one example of how my dad helped me build confidence in myself. He encouraged us in everything we did.

"When we were quite young, we didn't have much money, but we had a lot of love. If we really wanted something, but we knew we couldn't afford it, we didn't even ask. But if dad knew we wanted something special, he would love to surprise us by buying it for us. He would cut corners elsewhere just so he could see the look of delight on our faces.

"Dad could never bear to see someone in need and, during the years when I was growing up, we almost always had someone staying with us to help them get back on their feet. Many times dad would call my mom and ask her if she would put another plate on the table and asked if supper could be stretched, because someone who had stopped at the church or someone he had met somewhere, needed a good meal.

"Dad and mom never yelled at us and we kids never yelled in our home. We were all definitely disciplined, and I had my share of spankings but they were always in love. I was a stubborn little kid, and when mom used to spank me I would determine not to cry, and would laugh instead. But when my dad spanked me, it worked. I remember, though, that I would rather have a spanking and feel like I had paid for the wrongdoing, than to have my dad sit me down and talk about my actions. When we would talk, I would feel so bad for hurting my father. I would feel like I had really let him down. I always had a desire for my dad to be proud of me. I'm sure this feeling kept me, as well as my sisters and brother, from doing anything really wrong, because we so much wanted our mom and dad to be proud of us. Dad trusted and believed in all of us.

"One thing I loved while growing up was going on vacations as a family. A lot of friends thought it was old fashioned to do things or go places with your parents, but I loved it. As a family we just enjoyed being together. I remember one vacation in particular. We traveled down to California and stayed with my Uncle Al. He had a yacht and took us out on the ocean. It was a super neat time, just relaxing together as a family. On that same vacation, we went down to Tijuana, Mexico. I loved to watch my dad as he dickered with the shopkeepers trying to get better prices.

"Dad had a great sense of humor. When he heard something that struck him funny, he would close his eyes, lay his head back and roar with laughter. I loved to tell my dad jokes or do something funny so I could hear his infectious laugh.

"I remember one evening about a week before dad died, our family was all over at mom and dad's house relaxing in the family room. My dad really loved Ted's little girl, Cherry. She was such a happy baby. She was only about a year old and did not usually want to be held and loved by many people. For some reason, that night she climbed up into my dad's lap, gave him a love and sat there with him. She did this over and over, and I could see how happy he was to have her show him her love. After dad went to be with the Lord, that was one scene that kept coming back to me and touching my heartstrings.

"One thing that had a great impact on me was seeing the love displayed between my parents. They had tremendous respect and consideration for each other. I decided when I got married that I would not settle for anything less than that type of relationship.

"Throughout the years there were people who did not agree with my father, and some even tried to hurt his ministry. He did not react, instead he prayed for them, and tried to give them some extra love. He would not talk badly about anyone, although it must have hurt him to know some things which were said about him.

"Many people wondered why angels would visit my father,

and he wondered this too. I feel the Lord had the angels visit dad because he had shown himself to be a humble, good and faithful servant for the Lord. He was willing to do whatever was necessary to help people find the way to true joy and happiness in the Lord.

"It seems like dad could not keep from helping people. If a need was there, my dad was available—spiritually, physically, or financially.

"Our spunky red-haired mother shared in having a strong influence on the four of us. She didn't seem to let anything shock her. She rolled with the teenage storms we all went through, and would never make a big thing out of the fads and fashions as they would come and go. She seemed to remember how it felt to be young. The truth is my mother is the kind of person who will never grow old, because she is blessed with a young and joyful spirit."

Mom wraps up this chapter of the four Bucks:
"We were always in a building program trying to provide more room. Roland knocked on many doors and ministered to many people's needs so the churches grew.

"He was like a Rock of Gibraltar to me, especially when the children were sick. He often tried his hand at cooking. However, there was one concoction he made from leftovers that we named "Hash Malali," which the children ate only because they were hungry.

"I am so thankful for the solidarity and love that Roland gave to me and the family. There were some traumatic events in our lives—Sharon with rheumatic fever, the death of Terry, several heart attacks, and a heart arrest. Yet, through all of these times, he maintained a calmness that kept us from becoming distraught.

"Animals were an integral part of our lives. Roland loved them, and passed that love onto all our children. Charm especially seemed to always be bringing home some kind of animal life. One day near Easter time, I returned to find a big, fat, green rabbit in a cage in the living room! The kids named the rabbit Sebastian. Sebastian loved Roland and would thump along behind him when he would take an evening stroll around the neighborhood. What a sight! Charm also brought a baby duck home from the fair that followed her like a puppy. When she went upstairs, he would stand on the main floor and cry because he had been left behind.

"She also got a lizard at the fair. When it was time to go to school, she pinned him to her bedspread. While she was gone, our cat found the lizard, and when Charm came home from school, she was horrified to find the cat sitting on the bed purring and smiling, and only the tail left pinned to the spread. Charm carried the tail around in a box for a long time. She even tried to trade the tail to a friend for a live lizard!

"Sharon was a lover of dogs. I was always fearful that she might be bitten, for whenever she saw a dog, the scroungier the better, she had to love that dog. Amazingly she was never bitten.

"When we first moved to our present home, Ted and my husband brought home a Great Dane. I thought, "Oh, no! It's like having a pony in the house." She stayed, however, and is a real comfort to me now, because she was so much a part of my husband's life. She would go with him to the office every day.

"Can you imagine, a dog in church? She has become so much a part of our church family that people ask for her if she isn't around. One time when I was out of town, someone forgot to take her home. In the prayer service when they asked for those with needs to come forward, one of the first ones down to the front was Queenie. She was taken out as quickly as she came in.

"Another time when my husband and I were gone on a trip, she went into the first-grade class. There she was, ears drooping, head hanging low, big brown, sad doggy eyes, with her tail between her legs. Nothing could have looked sadder. One of the first graders said, "Queenie looks depressed. Let's pray for her!"

"Roland was kind and loving, but firm in discipline. In our first home in Boise we had a space down by the furnace which was almost like the old cellars. When Roland started removing his belt because they had been disobedient, the children knew what was coming—down to the cellar. It didn't happen often, but enough for our children to learn respect for their parents. Because of this training, the children have grown into adults who love and respect their parents. The closeness of our family is a priceless treasure in my heart.

15
TIME TO BUILD AGAIN

The church on Latah that had seemed too big sixteen years before, had been stretched, added onto, remodeled, but finally once again daddy was faced with the delightful problem that there were very few square feet left for expansion. The church was completely filled with about 600 people.

Daddy and the board of the church began to pray for direction. He took a week off and went up to a cabin in McCall, Idaho, to meditate and pray and set some goals. The Lord gave him direction as to what He wanted to accomplish through the ministry of Central Assembly.

The following is an excerpt from the Pastor's Report dated January 17, 1973:

"I would like to share with you some of the goals which I believe God has included in His plans for Central Assembly in the not too distant future. I see facilities geared to meet the present and future needs of this vigorous church. A worship center with ample seating for reasonably projected growth with a platform stage area built around the needs of our expanding choir and music ministry. Facilities and equipment for the care and training of babies and pre-school children, not only on Sunday, but specialized care during the week for children of working mothers. . . also for possible kindergarten or lower grade-school use.

"In addition to this I see in the future of this church a recreation area for use by all ages. Included in this projected outreach of our church may well be apartments for those in retirement or in need of emergency housing . . . not to forget facilities for kind Christian care for the ill and bedfast. Yes, I see this church as the center of life and activity for the families associated and for those God brings our way so that we need not look beyond ourselves for the answer to our temporal and spiritual needs. Truly a great door is open. This is our day. We cannot afford to let it pass but will advance until He comes."

Daddy and mother began looking for some property. They really had fun driving around Boise together, prayerfully seeking just the right spot for the new church which would be a Christian Life Center. The Lord had so impressed on daddy the importance of the whole man, body, soul and spirit, and he wanted this new facility to meet the needs of the whole person.

They found some property near a freeway that seemed ideal. The board was happy with it, but the more daddy prayed about it, the more uncomfortable he felt with it. He told mother that "It has the smell of death on it!" Because of this, the board delayed any action on this property.

One night about eleven daddy told mother that he just had to go out and drive around. He was gone for several hours. He told mother when he returned that he had begun to pray and drive. Finally he ended up by some land that seemed to be way out from the city center, yet it had a good feel about it. There were seventeen acres of good land on a well-traveled road.

A few days after daddy found this property, the owner of the first property near the freeway died. If they had gone ahead and purchased that land, the estate could have been tied up in litigation for a long time.

The new spot on Fairview had been sought after by many

hopeful buyers throughout the years, but the owner just hadn't felt like selling. When he was approached about selling his land to Central Assembly, however, God quickened his heart, and he consented to sell at a modest price compared to what he could have been paid for the land.

In researching the land before finalizing the purchase, the board learned that the flow of the city was going in the direction of the property. They were able to purchase seventeen acres, and take out an option on seventeen more.

God continued to add His blessing to the congregation as they moved forward for Him, by helping them to sell the Latah church to a business conglomerate. This released some much needed funds for the new project.

What an exciting time! The plans that were drawn up appeared huge. An auditorium to seat 1500 seemed almost too big for this congregation. The foyer that was included in the plans seemed absolutely mammoth. Some of the people began to complain and say, "Why do we have to build a new church, we're satisfied with things the way they are!" But Daddy was being directed by the Holy Spirit and he took as his model Nehemiah from the Old Testament, who told the would-be detractors from the job of rebuilding the wall, "I'm not coming down from the wall to fight with you! God has given me a job and I am going to do it!"

The building was completed in record time for a structure of this size. John Hisel, the general contractor for the project, shared with me another glimpse into what kind of person my daddy, Pastor Roland Buck, was:

"I'll never forget the time when we were building the church, and my carpenters had built the foundation forms to the prayer room about two feet out of square. As the general contractor, it was my responsibility to make sure everything was mechanically and structurally correct. But in my own checking of the job, I missed the error. We were to pour the concrete at 8:00 A.M. the next morning. Unknown to me, pastor, in his general observation of the job, had seen the mistake. Instead of jumping on me or my carpenters about an error which could have been very costly, and causing us to lose face, he was on the job site at seven o'clock the next morning.

"As I was preparing the day's work, he said, 'Say, John, I haven't had a personal tour of the job lately. Do you think you could update me on our progress?' I said, 'Sure, pastor, things are just great. I'll show you around.' As we toured the job site he asked me questions about different things. Then he led me to the prayer room, and asked questions about how we built forms, and what was involved in pouring the concrete. This caused me to look closely at our layout, and immediately I saw that the forms were out of square. I excused myself, *fast,* and went to cancel my concrete order. As I hung up the phone, I realized what your dad had done. He had allowed me to discover my own mistake and retain my dignity as a leader of the job. When I got back to where we had been talking, he had disappeared. At that point he had won my undying loyalty. The church was built in eleven months, which was almost unheard of for a project of that size.

"Pastor Buck had a unique ability to lead people. There was never any strain or manipulation. He had a way of making you want to follow and be a part of what he was doing. He made you want to work hard on the common goal.

"Another thing that meant so much to me personally was that in our board meetings, he never discussed difficulties that members of the church got themselves into, or allowed us to discuss people's problems. He handled all of those himself. So, when I met someone in the hall at church, who maybe had a problem, I could shake his or her hand and never be embarrassed, and they could hold their head up high, knowing that what they had entrusted with him, he would never divulge.

"This to me is a sign of true leadership—helping people attain their goals, without elevating yourself! This was my pastor."

16
QUEENIE

If only Queenie could talk, imagine the things she could tell us! Queenie is a beautiful Great Dane, now eight years old. She was with daddy during most of his meetings with the angels. She has been privileged to have her ears scratched by these heavenly beings.

Daddy loved animals, especially dogs. Queenie was sort of a birthday present to my mother. Sort of a birthday present because she came to live in the Buck household on my mother's birthday, and how could mother not accept her birthday gift? Mom liked little dogs, and probably would have loved a toy poodle, or a little house dog. The family already had a dog named Bronco who was part Dachshund, and part Cocker Spaniel. The part that was Dachshund was the short legs and long, long body. The rest of Bronco was Spaniel. He was a funny looking and an endearing dog.

Daddy walked in with Queenie, who at two months, towered over Bronco. Although Queenie was already quite large, she only knew that she was a puppy, and as such, wanted to be loved.

Daddy said, "Charm, here's your birthday present!" Queenie took one look at my mother and fell in love. She tore across the room and leaped into her lap, which wasn't

109

nearly big enough to hold her. Mother gingerly patted Queenie on the head, as she laughed and said, "Honey, this is not my birthday present!" All of us kids were chuckling as we watched Queenie trying to snuggle up on mother's lap, an impossible feat! She jumped down and bounded around the room, making herself at home. Mother did have some other birthday presents, by the way, but Queenie was there to stay!

Queenie grew into a beautiful, sleek dog. She and daddy became constant companions. Whenever you saw daddy out walking, close behind was a beautiful Dane. Queenie made a path from the parsonage, across the fields to the church. Daddy began to walk to church with Queenie, following her path as it zigzagged through the tall grass.

Queenie spent many hours in daddy's office as he prayed with people and counseled with them. When some people would be fearful of the big Dane, we staff members would smile and tell them not to be because, "Queenie is a Christian, and helps pastor pray with people!"

She also adopted me, and if daddy was out of town, Queenie would mournfully come to my office to lay in the sun.

She was very gentle, and loved children. When Marantha School came into existence through Central Assembly, Queenie was in heaven with all the children to play with. She became the school mascot, and the team name became the "Great Danes."

Queenie even received her own activity card with her picture on it, entitling her to free access into all the school activities.

One of the things that Queenie loved about the school year was the different lunches the kids would bring. They soon learned not to stand with their arms down if they had a sandwich in their hand, because Queenie would think it was for her and would very quietly help herself. Many times you could hear one of the little kids saying with childlike astonishment, "Teacher, Queenie ate my lunch!" Queenie would quietly slink around the side of the school and be gone.

After the book *Angels on Assignment* was published, Queenie was famous. Everywhere daddy went to speak, people—especially children—would ask, "How's Queenie?"

When my father went to be with the Lord, we all expected Queenie to quit eating and mourn until she died, because she loved her master so much. But perhaps the Father, who hears even the soft sound of a tiny little sparrow falling to the earth, whispered into her ear that it was okay, "her master was with God!" Queenie did not really mourn. Prior to his death, when daddy would be gone, Queenie wouldn't eat well. But this time, she continued to eat, and although it took her a little while to be really frisky, I really believe Queenie knows where her master is.

17
MUSIC, MUSIC, MUSIC

Daddy loved music. He had a choir in every church he pastored, and Central Assembly was no exception. Mother directed the choir for many years.

In 1965 there was a tremendous revival that swept our youth. Many were saved and baptized in the Holy Spirit. The first thing we young people wanted to do was find some way of sharing the new life we had found. We decided to form a choir, and share the life of Jesus through music. The choir was directed by one of the girls in the group, Gloria Locklear, and I became her assistant.

The church began advertising us as the Singing Ambassadors, and soon the city of Boise became aware of this turned-on, young, singing group.

Gloria directed the Singing Ambassadors for four years. During this time we made several record albums locally. Then Gloria met "Mr. Right" and was married. She and her husband moved away to attend college.

Several people worked with the choir on a part-time basis following Gloria's departure, but with the type of ministry it had become, it really needed a full-time director.

Daddy and the board discussed who should become the new director for the group which had become such a vital arm of Central Assembly. They came up with a list of several people including me. Daddy okayed every name on the list, but told the board members he wasn't sure about me. He didn't want the fact that we were related to cause problems for me if I was chosen as director. Because of my name being on the list, daddy stepped back from making the final decision, and told the board members to make this selection a real matter of prayer. If they felt the direction of the Lord on any of these names, including his daughter, Sharon, he would accept their choice as being from the Lord.

The board members did make this a matter of prayer and fasting. Several of them prayed for many, many hours. They felt that their choice was very important because of the tremendous impact the choir had made in the lives of the young people and also in the ministry of the church.

Early one morning my phone rang. It was one of the board members asking me to meet with the board that evening. I had butterflies all day, and I, too, asked the Lord for direction, especially because I was now married with two young children, ages three months and fourteen months.

That evening I felt a quickening in my heart as the board members told me that after much prayer, they felt very definitely led of the Lord to ask me to be the director.

I did not have a strong musical background, but I did have a great love for music, and a real desire to serve the Lord. I decided that if the Lord wanted me, then together we could do anything.

I was so very close to my dad in my growing-up years, and had absorbed so much of his love for people, I had the priceless opportunity now, to put into action all that I had learned from all those years of association with my father.

First of all, the twenty-six young people who had stayed with the group during this transition time got together with me and we prayed up a storm asking God for divine direction.

Next, I wrote every young person who had ever come through the doors of Central Assembly, and invited them to a planning meeting. Imagine my excitement when fifty-six young people showed up.

Daddy gently guided me and with the Lord on our side, the group began to come together once again into a dynamic tool for the Lord. Daddy understood that young people often like different types of music other than the established music of the church. So although he encouraged a balance, he allowed the group to sing songs full of the life and joy of youth.

My brother, Ted, had two friends, identical twins, who played football with him. They were big handsome guys. Through his witness, and his invitation to a special youth revival, these two young men accepted the Lord. They had become part of the choir several years after the group was formed. Greg had a deep bass voice, and Jeff played the drums. When I began to direct the choir, my brother Ted and these two young men really got behind me and supported my efforts by their faithfulness to the ministry. Jeff totally gave his drumming ability to the Lord and to the choir.

Jeff and Greg spent a lot of time in our home because of their friendship with Ted, and their involvement in the music ministry. They both shared with me their special love for Pastor Buck:

JEFF: "My first exposure to Pastor Buck was while sitting around the dinner table with Ted and my brother.

"The special thing about him was his willingness to listen to you while you were trying to sort things out, and not just telling you what to do. He didn't attack what you were believing as a young Christian. He sought to understand it, and then reflect why he didn't feel the same way, discussing the pros and cons. When you left, you would know where he stood, but he didn't berate how you believed.

"He was really low key, and one of the valuable things about him was that he didn't say, 'Let me tell you what the Bible says' and just give a pat answer to the need in your life, but he would help you search out what you were feeling, and would give God some working room.

"In my sophomore year of college, I was trying to find what direction my life was going to take. I needed some time to be alone, so Pastor Buck let me stay in the church for three or four days. He understood that I needed solitude more than talking. There's nothing quite so wonderful and moving as praying in a dark, empty church at night, just being able to be alone and to worship, praise, and sing to the Lord. It was what I needed most.

"Pastor Buck never pushed, but he tried to genuinely understand. After all was said and done, he would step aside and say, 'From here on in it's not my job, it's God's!'"

Jeff is now a Doctor in Human Factors Psychology. He is a Project Engineer at Hughes Aircraft Company in California.

GREG: "Ted brought my brother and me to church. Pastor Buck seemed like he was always interested in us. It wasn't a superficial thing as if he was asking you about yourself because it was the thing to do. There was a genuine interest. You could relate to him because he was such a masculine guy. He had a real strength, yet he had a deep compassion. He really cared about the people he was working with, and cared about what was important to you. It's hard to describe Pastor Buck, to put into words your feelings about somebody like him. His voice was deep and resonant, yet there was a mellowness and compassion that came through clearly. You could look at his eyes, that were deep and dark, quiet, yet powerful. You didn't have to put on pretenses. You knew you could be yourself around him, relax and feel at ease. It seemed he knew what you were like anyway.

"When he died it was like losing part of my family. It was a shock. It was as if there were a solid piece of your life that's been there providing a stability and suddenly it's gone! I had to do a tremendous amount of adjusting after his death. Ted

115

was a lot of help to me. He took it better than I did. I fell apart.

"When he was visited by angels, I thought if it had happened to anyone else, I couldn't believe it, but with him, it had to be true. That's the way I felt, because I knew him well enough, and knew that he was so down to earth, something like this had to be real."

Greg is a sales representative for a pharmaceutical company.

Soon after I began directing the group, I became dissatisfied with just drums and piano, and I asked the Lord for a good trumpeter. The Lord answered my prayers by directing me to the very best, a talented young musician and trumpeter, Dan Smith. Dan shares the story in his own words of our meeting.

DAN: "I was confronted with the possibility of going to Central by my roommate. He had gone to a Sunday night service the week before, and said that there was a good youth group there. The next Sunday morning I visited the service and have been going ever since.

"The vivacious people my age made the whole idea seem very enticing, and as an added bonus, lo and behold, there was a forty-voice youth choir that sang just my kind of music!

"A week and a half later, Sharon White came sneaking around my dog food aisle at Buttrey's Supermarket and asked me if I would be interested in playing trumpet with the choir. Sharon had been told by a friend that I played trumpet, and was just back from college and available. Sharon didn't know that I had already visited Central Assembly. I told her I would try to come to the next Wednesday practice.

"Wednesday came, and my boss would not let me leave two hours early. For some reason, going to this practice meant a lot to me. I was excited about it so I went in spite of my boss. June 4, 1970, was my first day with the choir, and the past ten years have been a blessing for me in seeing the choir grow and develop and in seeing many lives changed for

Christ. That day in June, thanks to my boss, was also the last day of my grocery store career!

"Pastor Buck wholeheartedly endorsed the work of the choir. He saw it as a ministry that reached a certain segment of people that possibly would not be reached in any other way. It had grieved me so to see some men of God put music off in a corner. But he saw and felt the worship and praise in inspired gospel songs. He realized the joy and happiness that could be received. This quality in Pastor Buck was probably the backbone of the Singing Ambassadors' long-running success and acceptance!"

Dan was really special. He had the technical knowledge that I lacked, and although he was one of the top musicians in Boise, and later would travel with the Spurrlows, he caught the vision of our choir ministry, and added his expertise which was far above the talent in the choir. His trumpet added a new dimension to the sound. Soon other musicians were attracted by the opportunity to play music for Jesus that appealed to young and old alike.

The band grew and soon there were three outstanding trumpeters, along with trombonists, bass guitar, guitar, flute and drums. Dan's work was cut out for him. He and I agreed that although the choir was made up of people whose only requirement to sing was that they love Jesus, the band should have a standard of excellence. He began to arrange music to accompany the choir. With the new accompaniment, the sound became even more exciting and dynamic. The praise songs were powerful, and the worship intense.

The choir and band were able to perform at the Idaho State Fair in 1975 at six o'clock during the dinner hour, a time when hardly anyone was there. The group went over so well, however, that for the last five years, we have been given our own stage at 9:00 P.M. when hundreds of fairgoers are pouring into the fairgrounds. Beneath a 12-foot high backdrop that says, "UP WITH JESUS," we have been allowed the freedom of singing for Jesus with no holds barred. As people have stopped to watch and listen, they cannot believe that this is a local group, and many, many people have found Jesus as a result of the seeds planted through this musical presentation.

The Singing Ambassadors started a "Hot Dog for Jesus" booth to earn money for equipment. We also bought muppets, and added a regular muppet show to our Idaho State Fair outreach.

Daddy was thrilled as he watched the group grow into such an exciting ministry. He felt that we ministered right along with him every Sunday morning and evening. He encouraged the Singing Ambassadors, as he did all of us children when we were growing up, that all these young people were in partnership with him. He saw many, many people find Jesus as a result of the two-pronged thrust of the anointed music ministry, combined with the richness of what he shared directly from God's heart.

The Singing Ambassadors worked together to produce Christmas and Easter musicals, that soon had to be expanded to five presentations to handle the standing-room-only crowds.

One very special Sunday will never be forgotten by any of us. It was my daddy's last Christmas season.

It was the Sunday before Christmas and we had planned to sing the "Hallelujah Chorus" to excite people about our presentation the following week. However, as the time to sing that morning drew closer, I began to get cold feet, wondering if the choir was ready to sing that song. Finally I whispered in daddy's ear that we weren't singing the 'Hallelujah Chorus" after all because I wasn't sure the choir could do our best without several more rehearsals.

He really startled me by saying, "Honey, I *want* you to sing that song this morning. You see I had another visit from Gabriel last night, and he told me that God was sending him to the service this morning. I told him that the choir was going to be singing the "Hallelujah Chorus."

I got goosebumps, and standing in front of the choir, I

whispered to them why we were *still* going to sing this beautiful, triumphant song. Some of them could hear, but most of them could not. As we began to sing, however, an anointing from heaven fell as never before. Some of them could hardly stand. We sang the "Hallelujah Chorus" far beyond our own ability that morning.

After the service two families, who were visiting Central for the first time, waited to ask daddy a question. They did not know each other, and they were waiting on different sides of the platform. The first family told him that they were visitors and wondered about the tall bright light on the platform that moved back and forth in front of the choir while we were singing. Later, the other family asked daddy the same question. He was able to tell them both that there was a heavenly visitor in the service that morning.

You can imagine the thrill we choir members felt as we learned of the heavenly visitor, and the confirmation by these two families. We understood then the reason for the overpowering anointing that we had experienced as we sang.

Through the years of ministry with the choir, the Lord has sent exceptional pianists to work with me. To each of them the Lord has given the vision of what He can accomplish through anointed music. Wanda Lehmkuhl worked with me for the first four years. When she had to move, the Lord immediately brought in Sheri Shirley and her family. These dedicated people gave unselfishly of time and prayer to this ministry. When Sheri's husband was transferred, the Lord had already provided an extra special replacement. Linda Buck, Ted's wife, became not only a sister-in-law, and special friend, but her excellent talent on the piano, combined with her creativity, adds a tremendous zest and energy to the music ministry as she and I work together.

Daddy had the privilege of seeing me and my husband, Alan, join forces as Alan became the sound engineer. Alan also uses his artistic abilities in the many productions, publicity for the choir and the numerous outreaches of the church.

Daddy guided me into some principles that are the basis for the music ministry of the Singing Ambassadors:

1. The choir and band minister first to God.
2. Secondly to each other.
3. And the direct overflow will be ministry to the congregation.

Captain Green
and one of his grandchildren

Hoyt and Daisy Buck

Gladys, Al,
Roland, Walt, Dot,
Margaret and George
1923

Walt, George, Al and Roland

Roland in College

Study time

Work
time

Granger, Wn.
Home of the Splashing Dust

Charm
'Spunky Redhead'

Honeymoon cottage

Union Gap, Wn.
First pastorate together

Dad, the new addition Sharon
& Mom
1943

Sharon at two . . .
bald as a billiard ball
soloist

Gooding, Idaho

Christmas 1945

Charm, Sharon, Mom,
Ted, Dad & Mimi
1954

21st & Alturas
First church in Boise

Sharon, Dad,
Mom, Mimi, Ted & Charm
1959

The 'Barn' . . . Latah Church

Groundbreaking ceremonies
for the new Christian Life
Center on Fairview 1972

First Service
in the sanctuary
1973

Present facility

Ted, Mom, Dad, Sharon, Marilyn, Charm

Our family

Dad and Mom 1979

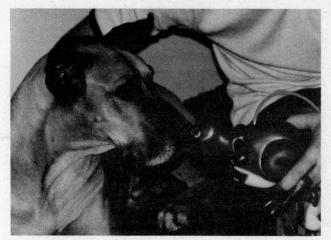

Queenie and 'Friend'

Queenie and Dad by the stream
behind the house

Autograph
time

One of many
interviews

"Angels on assignment"

Ted at tackle

Linda and Ted as pastors

The singing Ambassadors with living sound

Me, hard at work on this book

18
PASTOR BUCK AND THE KIDS

Daddy absolutely loved children! He was never too busy to talk with them. And he considered what they had to say as important as any adult. This truly endeared him to the children.

Jason was three and a half years old and extremely hyperactive. His mother had her hands full with three other children. One day, she and her husband decided to take Jason in to see my father. When he prayed for little Jason, they could feel the calming power of God go through that little body, relaxing those tight little muscles.

Jason did very well the next year and a half, but when he started kindergarten, hyperactivity again became a problem, especially in his dealings with other children. Jason's mother and teacher were at their wits' end. Since he was attending the Maranatha Kindergarten at Central Assembly, they decided to make an appointment for Jason to see daddy by himself.

Although my father was very busy, his counseling schedule alone sometimes amounting to 50 hours a week, he wasn't too busy to see this little boy.

After the first session, he scheduled from thirty minutes to an hour a week for Jason. A whole new world opened up to him because daddy began teaching this little five-year-old boy how to read. Once a week Jason would come into his office, and everytime he left, he was carrying a little tablet with his reading assignment on it. Daddy also shared with him what God was really like and taught him how to talk to God all by himself.

Jason became a new little boy, and was happy because my father called him his "little buddy."

One day Jason said, "Mom, Pastor Buck must be an awful lot like God!" She asked, "Why is that, honey?" He responded, "Because he loves us little kids so much!"

Daddy also had another little boy who was his "buddy." This little boy had a problem of being all brain and no brawn. Dad met with him once a week also, and worked with his muscles. He would give him a different kind of assignment, that of doing so many push-ups, sit-ups, or running so many miles as his homework. My father encouraged young and old to have a balance of body, soul and spirit.

A boxing ring in the church? Daddy decided to give the boys at Maranatha High School some boxing lessons, sharing with them some of the knowledge and skill he had developed in years past. At the same time, he would be able to gain a priceless rapport with these young men, and could incorporate some solid spiritual truths into their boxing lessons. He talked one of the gyms into loaning him good equipment. The boys loved it. Every Wednesday was their day, and they would never let their teacher forget them. All other appointments had to wait while he worked with his boxing class.

One night, visitors to the church were astonished to walk in and find a boxing ring set up in the middle of the foyer. My father and Pastor Mike, our youth pastor, were the referees, and the boxing class of Maranatha was having an exhibition.

One of the boys who was part of that class told me how daddy had called him into his office one day. He was scared, wondering what he had done. Dad did not beat around the bush. He told this young man that God had let him know some things he was doing in secret. The young man was really startled. He prayed with my father and he quit doing those things. Daddy continued to pray for him.

Several weeks before this book was written, this young man came to my office and shared that he had given his life completely over to the Lord. He was so thankful for the kind of pastor who cared enough to share himself with him and his friends.

Daddy had a terrific idea. Although he was putting in many, many hours already and Sunday was a big day, he decided that he wanted the chance to share with all the little kids in his church what God was really like. So every Sunday evening an hour before the service, he opened his office to "little kids only." His office would be crammed with several dozen children. He would teach them about the beautiful nature of God. He showed them how to pray for one another and led them in worship.

During one of these sessions, he talked about fear of the dark and noises at night. He told the children that the Bible says that the angels of the Lord encamp around those who love the Lord. He told them that when they heard creaking noises or scary sounds in the night, it was just the angels throwing more wood on their campfire.

He had a good chuckle about a week later when a mother called and told him her little boy had been trying to go to sleep the night before. It was a stormy night. The wind was howling and making the house creak with scary noises. Finally, her little boy called her and said, "Mom, I sure wish those angels would be a little more quiet. I can't get to sleep because they're making so much noise around their campfire!"

One day, Queenie stole the lunch of a little kid who was a little more resourceful than most. This young man decided to go straight to the top. He knocked on my dad's door. Daddy opened the door, and there stood a little boy who said, "Pastor Buck, Queenie stole my lunch." Dad said, "Well, we can't have that, can we?" That afternoon a very proud little guy went to lunch with his pastor at the drive-in down the street. Word got around, and pretty soon Queenie was having a field day with lunches "accidentally" left lying around. More and more kids were knocking on daddy's door with the sad story of Queenie stealing their lunches. He really got a chuckle out of this and said, "Those kids are sure smart little rascals, aren't they?" Actually, he really enjoyed taking these little ones to lunch once in a while.

The church had an excellent preschool day-care program. Every day at noon the little kids would line up and march over to the church where there was a dining room with tables just their size, right next to dad's office. Every once in a while, he would open his door when he would hear the children going to lunch, and when they would see him, they would say in their little voices, "There's Pastor Buck. Hi, Pastor Buck!" He would come out of his office and get down on one knee to talk to them, and they all would swarm over to him and have to have a hug.

His last Halloween, all the little kids in the preschool dressed up for a party. Pastor Buck was invited to come over and see all of them. They were so excited when he walked in. Everybody wanted him to see their costumes. He got down on one knee, and just like a signal had been given, the children formed a line around him and each one had to have an individual hug and show off their costume.

Daddy was a typical, proud grandfather. He loved his grandchildren. My daughter, Angie, was the first grandchild, and he thought she was the prettiest, most delightful little creature he had ever seen. "Nana" Buck, of course, shared these feelings totally. Eleven months later, I presented my father with a little grandson, Terry, and he thought his life was complete. Then nine days later, my sister, Charm, adopted a little boy, Bryan. Both grandparents were so thrilled and delighted, it was fun to see. That Sunday my dad's buttons just about popped as he said with great pride, "It isn't *every* man that can get three grandchildren in less than one year!"

When I was a young girl growing up, my father used to build me up. Now that I was a mother of two little babies, he would compliment me often on what a fine mother I had turned out to be. Even when I felt like I was the worst, witchy mother in the world, he would pat me on the back and say, "Honey, you're doing just great."

When the two little boy cousins, Terry and Bryan, and Angie got together, it was really something. When they were 3 and 4 years old I overheard the three of them telling some little kids who were acting up, "You had better be good, 'cause our grandpa is the boss of this church."

Daddy was absolutely delighted with his six grandchildren, my two, Angie and Terry, Charm's three, Bryan, Heather and Heidi, and Ted's little girl, Cherry. He felt they were the brightest, sharpest, little grandchildren ever born. He built up their self-esteem just like he did with all of us kids when we were growing up.

After daddy had gone to be with the Lord, my two children were saying their bedtime prayers. They were in separate bedrooms so they didn't hear each other. My heart was so touched as they both ended their prayers with, "And God, would you please tell grandpa we miss him and we still love him!"

When daddy went to be with the Lord, Mother received letters from many of his little friends. The following are some of these letters.

Dear Mrs. Buck

Pastor Buck was a great Pastor. Every time I said hi he would shake my hand. I'm glad he was my Pastor. I loved him very much.

Johnny Lammeet

Dear Mrs Buck, I love you much And
I liked your husband. Your husband once
gave me five dollars to buy my mom and
dad a Christmas presentd.

Love,
Heidi Wilson

Sister Buck,

I am really sorry about Pastor Buck
I really lovd him. He always new when
people had problems

He loved kids and always treated
them like grownups. But now

Hes gone to be where he always
to be and I can't wait till
I go to heaven and see
him

love in Christ   Chad Estes

Dear Mrs. Buck,

Mr. Buck was very nice. We will all miss him very much, but he went home to live with God. He is probely happer there.

He had so much love in his hart and I just loved him. He was so much like God. I was glad he baptised me and he did such a good job.

Queeny is so nice to I realy like him, but my dog does not, but I think it is because Muffy is so little and Queeny is so big.

❀

Love,
Andrea Arnold
4th grade girl

127

19
THE BOOK,
ANGELS ON ASSIGNMENT

One Monday morning my father walked into my office. This was not unusual because, although he was very busy, he would often take a few minutes out of his busy schedule, and he and Queenie would stroll down the hall to my office for a little chat.

That particular morning he threw me a bombshell. We were quietly discussing the services the day before, when in the same ordinary tone of voice daddy asked me a very extraordinary question. He said, "Honey, what would you say if I told you that I had a visit from an angel last Saturday night?" I said, "What?" He repeated, "I had a visit from an angel last Saturday night!" "Wow!" was my response! He asked, "Do you believe me?" I told him, "Of course I do!"

He then began to describe this incredible encounter. I literally hung on every word. I asked him when he was going to share this visit with the congregation. He said he didn't know, and wondered if people would believe him. I told him, "Of course they will!" He then dropped another bombshell, as he said very softly, "He was the angel, Gabriel!"

My mouth really fell open then. Tears began to stream

down his cheeks as he continued sharing with me the message the angel had brought from God. Tears filled my eyes too, as I listened to what my father was saying. He was a man who would never try to be flamboyant or lean toward the sensational just to reach people. He had steered a steady, middle-of-the-road course for many years, not following the different fads that would come and go as men were seeking their way in the new charismatic outpouring from God.

The supernatural work of God through my dad's life didn't begin with the angelic visitations. All through his ministry God would, at different times, let him know areas of need in people's lives as he would shake their hands following a church service. Or God would reveal someone to him as they were involved in something they wouldn't want anyone to know about. Daddy would either immediately go to that person, or tell them later, as God would direct. There were a lot of people who learned how much God cared about what they did or did not do, as He would reveal these things to Dad. God could trust dad with any information, because unless God released it in his spirit, *no one* else ever knew the secrets God had shown him other than the person involved. He always said that he felt the word of knowledge can be a dangerous thing in the hands of a careless person.

I remember when one of my good buddies was dating one of the girls in our youth group. They became engaged, and as the date for their marriage approached, dad wondered why the young man was avoiding him. One day I asked my buddy why he was avoiding dad. He said, "Well, sometimes my fiancee and I get kind of involved on Saturday night, and I know that God knows, but I just don't want God to tell Pastor Buck!"

Dad's first "out of body" experience was a visit to God's throne room. One Saturday night in January, 1977, about ten-thirty in the evening, daddy was seated at his desk meditating and praying and preparing his heart for Sunday.

His head was resting in his arms on the desk, when suddenly without any warning he was taken right out of the room, and he heard a voice say, "Come with me into the throne room where the secrets of the universe are kept!" Immediately he was in God's throne room. While he was there he learned many things from God himself. In fact, God gave him a paper that had a list of 120 things that would occur in the two years that were to follow. On that list were things that related to his ministry, names of people, places and also events relating to world happenings. This visit to the throne room is described in detail in daddy's book. As he was coming back from this visit and as he entered the room, he saw himself from behind, and saw his body with his head down on his desk. He told the Lord, "I didn't realize I was that white!" He hadn't seen the back of his head that much, and he hadn't realized before how white his hair was becoming. When he sat up, he found the paper from heaven still in his hand. As he shared this with me, I can't really express the feeling in my heart of awe and wonder. He told me that he laid the paper on his desk. When he went home he was white as a sheet. When my mother asked him what was wrong, he could not tell her at first.

The next morning when he went back to his office to look at the paper, all that was laying where it had been were very light fluffy ashes. He left them there all morning. His secretary, Jo Ann Marsden came in and saw the ashes but she didn't disturb them, although she wondered what they were.

Finally at the end of the day he scooped the ashes into an envelope not wanting to attach any special reverence to them other than that they were heavenly ashes. When I saw the ashes the next day it was very strange because they did not leave a sooty mark on the envelope. They finally evaporated completely leaving the envelope just like new.

Before his death, all 120 predictions had been fulfilled. About a year and a half after his throne room visit, he received the first message, through angelic messenger, from the Father.

Altogether, he was privileged to experience 27 angelic visitations between June 18, 1978, and October 13, 1979. Eighteen of these are described in the book, *Angels on Assignment*. Portions of the nine visitations which occurred following the publishing of that book will be shared in the next few chapters.

Early one morning the Holy Spirit told my dad to write the following:

"Write, preserve the words which I have spoken to you. They shall become a light to many. I will not only minister through you, but will accompany these words, and give them life wherever sent, even as I have already given wings to My messages brought to you by the angel of the Lord. Fear not to speak in His name, for the words I give are not your words, but His words, and are established forever. Are they not found in His eternal living Word? Long closed doors of many peoples and nations will be penetrated by these words of life. I command the hosts of the Lord who have been sent forth for this hour to hasten the gathering together unto Him a people for His Name, and to prepare them for that great day of the Lord. They will both precede and follow these words from the Father to make ready the people, to scatter forces of darkness, and to gently care for the multitudes who will hear."

Daddy had this promise from the Lord, so he never tried in any way to help God get the message out that He told him to share with the world. He simply preached the messages to his congregation and left the rest up to God.

Tapes of the messages he preached to his congregation began to circulate all over the United States. Soon the tapes were being duplicated and sent all over the United States and Canada, and to many countries around the world. Requests came from people who were hungry to hear the messages straight from God's heart, as brought to my father by divine messenger.

The tapes finally reached Charles and Frances Hunter through some friends and their hearts were thrilled and their spirits quickened by the tremendous messages they heard. God's plan for getting His message out was unfolding through the obedience of the Hunters in responding to the urgency of this message.

Charles and Frances contacted daddy and their spirits witnessed his genuineness as they spent time sharing with him.

These dedicated servants of God, worked day and night for the next few months to edit the messages from the tapes. The manuscript flew back and forth between Houston and Boise, and finally on July 5, 1979, the book was completed, and ready for distribution in bookstores throughout the United States.

Daddy began to get calls from many places to speak. Following the leading of the Lord, he traveled extensively in the months that followed, sharing in large auditorium meetings, TV programs and in small fellowships.

People everywhere were finding Jesus. Hundreds of thousands found new hope through the beautiful Bible truths illuminated by divine messenger, and shared through the book and tapes.

Over and over daddy pointed people *to Jesus.* He told them that every message brought by angelic messenger exalted Jesus by reminding them what the sacrifice of Jesus meant to a lost world. Through this sacrifice, men and women once again could be reconciled with the Father.

The enemy of our souls could not stand to see so many people finding Jesus, and he began to stir up controversy and even hate.

A sign on the front of the church with daddy's name on it was vandalized and torn down. He then received an anonymous phone call from a man who said, "If you don't stop preaching the messages from the angels, I'm going to bash your head in, just like I did that sign!"

God suddenly showed dad what the man who was calling looked like as well as another man who had taken part and was listening to the call on another extension. God showed him the kind of truck they were driving when they damaged the sign, the license number, their address, even the clothes they had on at the time of the phone call. He called them both by name, and told them the information that God had showed him. Both men began to cry out to God over the phone, and daddy had the privilege of praying with them.

Another time he received a call from a woman who was nearly hysterical. Her husband had left the house with a gun, planning to shoot my father because of the tremendous change in the lives of his sons, who had accepted Jesus through reading the book, *Angels on Assignment*. The man never arrived, and daddy just kept on preaching the love of Jesus.

In some cities where he was asked to speak, both Satan-worshipers and Christians planned to picket the meetings. However, God always worked it out so they failed! God had something He wanted to accomplish, and nothing and no one could stop it.

The Hunters also experienced some persecution, but they, too, had caught the vision of what God is doing in these last days, and they marched forward with a God-given boldness to fulfill their part in bringing this message to the world.

Daddy was told by divine messenger to ignore the thrusts that were being made at him and at the message contained in the book. The angel referred him to Isaiah 45:9, "Let the potsherd strive with the potsherds of the earth."

The prophecy has come true with regard to the book, *Angels on Assignment*. It has been published in nine languages, and has gone into many countries around the world. At this writing over 550,000 have been sold since it came out in July, 1979.

The question is asked many times, "Why did God send angelic visitors to Pastor Buck?" His answer to that was, "I don't know why. I probably wouldn't have chosen me if I were God! But God did choose me, and I am simply obeying Him!"

The book by Charles and Frances Hunter, as told to them by my father contains the message that God wants the world to know. In a nutshell, though, the following is the message that was given.

There is good news for you and your family in these last days! God has sent out a host of angels to push, prod, and do whatever is necessary to bring people to a point of choice in accepting what He has done for them through the sacrifice of Jesus. The angels aren't listening to any objections from the individual, and if they don't choose Jesus the first time, then the cycle will start all over again. Angelic forces are on the job.

If you don't know the Lord, and someone from your family is praying for you, you are highly favored of God. He has sent His angels to bring you to a point of choice, because God loves you so much!

The main focus of the messages brought by the angels over and over again is the sacrifice of Jesus. He bore the stroke of God's judgment in His own body. Because of this sacrifice, when men and women accept what He has done, they are restored to their original state of innocence in God's eyes. They are made just as though they had never sinned. They are not pardoned in God's eyes, because pardon means the records are still there, but they are justified which means made as though they have never sinned.

What does this mean to you? It means when you find Jesus, you are not an ex-alcoholic, or an ex-homosexual, or an ex-prostitute, but the blood of Jesus covers you, letting God see only the righteousness of Jesus when He looks at you. You are therefore restored to your original state of innocence, as clean and pure in the eyes of the Father as the day you were born. That's what atonement means to you.

Doesn't this make you want to accept the wonderful new life that God offers you through the sacrifice of His Son Jesus? Why not do it right now? Jesus said "If you call upon My Name, you will be saved!" Just say, "Jesus, I accept what You have done for me, I believe in You, and I want to be your child from now on. Thank You for loving me so much!"

You are now born into the kingdom with a new heart, a new hope and a new life.

Another very important part of what God wants the world to know is that believers will not be at the White Throne Judgment. That judgment is only for those who reject Christ.

When God gathers all His believers around the throne, it will be to say "thanks" for all those things they did to help lift the load for someone. The encouraging word you gave, the plate of cookies you baked, "just because." Things that perhaps in the eyes of the world weren't anything really special, but through God's eyes represented His love being beamed through you to a world that is so hungry and cold and longing for that gentle touch. God will not turn His spotlight on your life at that time looking for the things you did wrong, because all of your sins and failures are covered through the atonement of Jesus.

The angel summed it up this way, "The believers' judgment is not a dark night through which he must pass before he breaks into God's eternal day, but a day in which God has chosen to thank His people!"

20
'TILL DEATH DO US PART

The main theme of the message brought to my Father by angelic messenger was the sacrifice of Jesus. God also shared with dad that one of His highest priorities—one of the closest things to God's heart—was the family.

With God's aid and grace, daddy had put many families back together through the years and he cherished his own family so much.

The next story is representative of the many people whose marriages were touched by God through the yielded ministry of my father. The first part of this story of Jim and Susan Olson was told in the book *Angels on Assignment*. In brief, Jim was number thirty-four on the list of 120 events, people, and dates that dad brought back with him from his visit to God's throne room.

Jim had sold out his life to Satan as a satanic priest. The Lord had given dad his name and even let him see Jim. On God's designated date, he came to the church and daddy recognized him, greeted him, and told him to come into his office. God saved him, blotted out all of the old evil that was in him, and gave him new hope and new victory.

Soon after, dad received this letter from him. Here are some excerpts. "As I related my life to you on April 9, 1977,

136

you didn't seem surprised at anything I said, it was as if you already knew. I discovered later that you did, because my name was on a list you had received from the throne room of Almighty God. You had been expecting me and it was no surprise to you that I accepted Jesus as my Lord and Savior.

"My life had been a series of ups and downs. I was raised in a parsonage and had been to the altar many times, but somehow I never completely surrendered. I became a medium and minister holding seances and giving readings. Controlled by demons, I had sunk as low as a man can go.

"As I tried to break away from this life, I lost my home, my dignity, and then my family. I had no place to go! My home became infested with rats that could not be killed! I called my mom and dad in Idaho and found that they still loved me. I left the spiritualist center and came to Idaho . . . and like the prodigal son . . . was welcomed home. In a short time, the Lord gave my family back to me and my wife and I took a trip to Hawaii. We met a couple there from Boise who invited us to your church . . . PRAISE THE LORD!

"There is a white flag that now stands in my office. It reads . . . . I HAVE SURRENDERED." (signed by Jim Olson)

However, Jim and Susan's story did not end there. As Jim shared with me the rest of the story, I realized that God's tremendous love for all of us, no matter where we are or what we have done, is illuminated to us once again, as Jim recaps the miracle-working power of God in his life and in his marriage in spite of his failures.

The following is taken from our interview: "We went along for awhile doing great. We were witnessing, but we wouldn't believe in the Holy Spirit. When I heard people talking tongues, or when I heard prophecy, it scared me to death because of my past involvement with the occult. This worried me so much, that finally Susan and I stopped coming to church. Then we started drinking again, and after all the evidence of the supernatural power of God in our lives, we split up and I moved in with another woman. Normally, this would have destroyed a pastor who had received a list from heaven with the name James Olson on it combined with God showing him everything about me. It should have totally blown his faith in God. A guy comes in, gets saved, his story is written in a book, and then he's right back into what he came out of. But Pastor Buck never gave up. He told me later, "I believe God. God had told me about you, but it's His business and He'll handle it." During this split-up, Susan was baptized in the Holy Spirit. She really began praying for me in the Spirit, but I had given up. This had been my final commitment, and I couldn't keep it. Pastor Buck told Susan, "I've never seen as much faith as you have! When God releases Jim from you, you'll know it!"

"I remember one night, I was drunk and called her from a bar. She took authority in the Holy Spirit and said, "Jim, I want you to come home!" And I did! I got in my car, but I told God, "Okay, God, You're going to have to watch me because I'm going to push the gas to the floor, and not stop until I get home!" When I pulled in I was a mess.

Susan persuaded me to come and see pastor, and you know, he loved me just as much in that messy condition as the first time he saw me. He never condemned me. I had made up my mind that I was through, but I had come to see pastor because I figured I owed him that much respect. We talked awhile, then he asked me if I would do something for him before I left. I loved him so much I said I would. He said, "Would you pray for Susan?" I couldn't believe my ears. I had told God that I didn't want anything more to do with Him, and Pastor Buck wanted me to pray for my wife! The authority of that man was such that I did.

"Well, I moved back home, but I was so messed up, a jangle of nerves, sick of sin, I wanted to kill myself, but I was afraid of going to hell. I was sure that I had committed the unpardonable sin. We once again found ourselves in pastor's office. I said, "Okay, pastor, I don't know what you can do!" He sent Susan from the room, then he laid hands on me and through the name of Jesus cast out three demons. I started laughing with joy, the tears running down my cheeks.

I could not stop. I was free. From that moment I started completely over, my sins forgiven.

"A few weeks later, at an altar service, I remembered pastor often saying, 'Just look up into Jesus' face and smile!' So I looked up and said, 'God, You've got to do something for me . . . give me something!' BAM! I was baptized in the Holy Spirit like someone dropped a tub of hot water all over me. From that time, nearly two years ago, until right now, I've had ups and downs, but I've never broken my commitment nor have any desire to because I've been saved and baptized in the Holy Spirit. I'm glad Pastor Buck lived long enough to see me grounded. I never met an individual who influenced my life like Pastor Buck. Not because he was a Christian, but because he was so solid. He wasn't a namby-pamby man. He was a man's man, but he had the gentleness of Christ. He acted more like Christ than anyone I know. Pastor Buck knew where I was coming from. He taught me that when God looks down on me, He has to see me through Christ. He always said, 'You're gonna make mistakes, but God looks beyond the flesh, and looks down into the "want to" inside.' I always get excited when I tell people about my pastor and how he knew God. You know why he could preach God's nature? It's because he knew God's nature firsthand, and he knew it long before he had these visitations. That's why he was allowed to have them . . . because he knew what God was really like prior to this and believed it! To anyone who is skeptical at all, I know it's true. I was a part of it!"

21
MORE ABOUT ANGELS

Daddy had the unique privilege in this day and age of meeting personally Gabriel, the angel who dwells in the presence of God, Michael the great archangel, and ministering angels from different parts of the world. During his several visits to heaven, he was able to see the beauty of the worship angels as they praised and worshiped Jesus.

Here from daddy's tapes, in his own words, are some interesting insights about these heavenly visitors.

"I used to think that all angels looked alike. Every picture I saw of them made them look alike. I was surely surprised.

"The angel had visited with me twice in my bedroom, and all I had seen was his outline against the light coming from my yard. Even this was overwhelming. But one night I noticed a bluish light coming up from the staircase. I thought I had left a light on in one of the rooms downstairs, so I decided to get up and turn the light off. I got halfway down the stairs, and the stairway light came on. I looked up and saw two of the largest men I have ever seen in my life. My knees buckled and I started to fall down the stairs. It could have been partly fright, but not totally. There is such a radiation of power from these angels because they come

140

directly from God's presence. My reaction was similar to being slain in the Spirit.

"The spokesman reached out and took hold of me and my strength returned. Then he told me he was Gabriel, and introduced me to the angel with him, whose name was Chrioni. He was a warring angel who was assigned to travel with Gabriel at this time.

"I learned that no two angels look alike. They are all different sizes with different hair color and styles. Gabriel stands about 7'2" tall and has gold-blond hair. It's straight, and goes about halfway over his ears. It's kind of a nice style. He has a more slender build than Chrioni. Chrioni's hair was black and had big loose curls. They were both very handsome, and looked about twenty-five to thirty years old. Chrioni was about four inches taller than Gabriel, and if I saw a man this big, I would know that he weighed 400 pounds or more. Chrioni's voice was so full and deep, he would make Big John Hall sound like a tenor.

"The first time I saw these two angels, Gabriel was dressed in a silver-colored tunic and slacks with a tie lacing it at the neck. Chrioni was dressed the same only his shirt was brown. Their skin and clothing glowed with a heavenly radiance.

"I asked them, 'Why are you here?' Gabriel then began to share some more beautiful truths with me about God's care for the people that He had created.

"He told me that the Holy Spirit monitors the whole earth at one time, and picks up signals from everywhere. He can even hear the bird that falls, wherever it is. I knew this was true academically, but this truth really became real to me that night.

"Gabriel continued to share with me that the Holy Spirit had sensed a massive build-up of satanic forces that wanted to attack me, because of what God was doing through my ministry. He told me then that the Spirit not only monitors the whole earth, He's the one who sends out the orders to the angels to go and scatter the enemy forces.

"I was a little concerned then, because I didn't want them standing there talking to me if the enemy forces were going to attack, but they told me that they had already finished the job.

"I asked Gabriel then what it takes to get the Holy Spirit to send out these forces to help people. Was it in answer to a prayer for help?

"Gabriel said, 'No, if the Spirit waited until you knew about an attack, you'd already be in trouble! Twenty-four hours a day divine forces are on the job scattering the forces of the enemy in response to the Holy Spirit's directives as He senses the need.'

"Then Gabriel asked me to take a look out the window. I was amazed to see about one-hundred of these men, like the big warring angel Chrioni, standing in my driveway casually chatting with each other. It made me feel pretty good to know that God has ways and means of taking care of His people!

"I might note that to this point Chrioni had not spoken to me. I had heard him talking to Gabriel, but he spoke in a different language. Gabriel told me that the angels could only speak with people as God would give them permission. Later on during another visit, God did give Chrioni permission to talk with me, and he really had some interesting things to share.

"I asked Chrioni to tell me about some of his most exciting memories. One of the memories he mentioned reminded me of how old he must be since angels were created before the earth was formed.

"Chrioni told about the time he helped lead the Children of Israel out of the land of Egypt. He said, 'God gave us the right to punish the Egyptians and use any of God's weapons. We threw lightning bolts at them. We pulled the wheels off their carts.' He didn't actually say it was fun, but he did say this event was fixed in his mind because of the great deliverance of Israel when the sea was pushed back. Chrioni also said that the angels had orders to intervene, but not to interfere with what God was doing in man's normal course of life."

(Author's note: The full account of my father's conversation with Chrioni is related in *Angels on Assignment*.)

"Gabriel then shared with me that God has four different kinds of angels. There are ministering angels who live among the people. They ride in our cars, live in our homes, and are camped about us all the time. Their orders from God are to take care of us. They look just exactly like a human being. The only way you would know them would be if they disappeared in front of your eyes, or if you saw them do some super-human feat. There are more of these on the earth than there are human beings. Since they do not dwell in heaven, they do not have the glow that emanates from the angels who live in heaven.

"The next group of angels are the worship angels. Their function is to worship Jesus. When I was taken to heaven I saw these angels in action, and it was one of the most beautiful sights I have ever seen. These are the only angels with wings. There are six wings, however, they don't really look like wings because they are a filmy material. The worship angels put two wings over their faces as they bow down. There are two more that drape around their feet like a bride's train, and two short ones on their back. The cherabim and seraphim are a very high order of these worship angels, but they have the same type of wings and the same function. Lucifer was the archangel of the worship angels before his fall.

"The third type are the great warring angels. These angels come from the presence of God and therefore a strong glow radiates from their skin and clothing. I never get used to their presence although I am not afraid. The heavenly radiation from them saps my strength, and I start to fall until they touch me and pick me up. Then I am strong again. After they have gone there is such a tingling sensation in my legs that for some time afterward I do deep knee bends and run in place because there is such power it is hard to handle in these earthen vessels. Michael is the archangel of all the warring angels.

"Then there are the special forces which include the messenger angels God uses to bring announcements and messages to the world. They also work in various ways in the unfolding of God's plan. The messenger angels also dwell in the presence of God, and glow with that special heavenly radiance.

"Gabriel is the archangel of the messenger angels and his chief purpose is in the unfolding of God's plan, and in the closing of one chapter of time, and the opening of another. Every time he has been referred to in the Bible he has brought announcements of a new day dawning. After he told me what his function was, it made me wonder what he is doing down here now? Could it be that another chapter is about ready to close and another one open?

"After Gabriel had finished telling me about the angels, he said that the highest and greatest divine being, One far above the angels, the highest in all the courts of heaven is Jesus. At the name of Jesus ringing through heaven, every angel, regardless of their rank falls in worship before Him.

"I asked Gabriel about Jesus' return. He told me that the Father had given him access to all of the things in God's time line but this was one thing that the Father kept to himself. But he said, 'I *can* tell you this. There is more excitement and activity in the courts of heaven than there has been at any time since Jesus came the first time!'

"It was very interesting to me to note that the angels did not always wear the same garb. All their shoes are the same, however, They look like they are made out of copper or metal. When I watch them flex their shoes, I know that they could not be metal because the shoes are of a very, very flexible substance.

"The bone structure of the eyebrows of the angels who live in heaven seems to be a little bit higher and more arched than those of a human being. Their eyes seem not colored

red like fire, they are dark, but they seem almost like rays. They are penetrating and to look at them is almost like looking into a pool of fire. It's not scary because you can almost feel their compassion as they are looking at you. They do not look inhuman. I have never seen a bearded angel that dwells in heaven. Agewise, they look like young men twenty-five to thirty. Michael looks about forty.

"The ministering angels I have seen look just like human beings, as I said before. The worship angels look like a broad variety of people, men, women, boys and girls, even some that look like small children.

"About two o'clock one Monday morning, I saw one of the most awesome sights I have ever seen. Every time God has revealed himself through the angels, it has been tremendous, but this seemed to be still more staggering because I felt the tremendous importance of what God is doing today in using Boise as a touchdown point for his divine messengers, and sharing with me a message for the world.

"I had heard something downstairs, so I went down. There in my living room I saw the great warring angel, Chrioni, and three other 'General angels,' if you can use that term, or 'Captains' of the hosts of heaven. I could hear them receiving messages from the Holy Spirit and sending out commands.

"Gabriel met me at the foot of the stairs, and took me into my family room. He told me that because of what God was doing through me, the princes of darkness had been gathered together and brought to this area for this particular time to try to delay and hinder the work of God. He said the Holy Spirit knew the way the enemy is working because he knows he has only a short time left. God had therefore sent Michael to my home that morning. I had never seen Michael before, but Gabriel introduced me to him.

"Michael's countenance was more fierce than Gabriel's, however, I could still sense the compassion and love and the nature of Jesus in him. He had strong, chiseled features. His eyes were like pools of fire. He was dressed like Gabriel with

145

a white tunic and a wide gold belt around his waist. The tunic had kind of a gold embroidery on it. His hands and arms were like someone with a deep tan, almost like burnished brass.

"Gabriel reminded me of the story in the Old Testament in Daniel 10, where Gabriel was delayed in bringing an answer to Daniel from the Lord by the princes of darkness, so God sent Michael to help Gabriel, and he has such power that it only took him to scatter the enemy so that the message could get through.

"There was a real spiritual battle going on, and the command post was in my living room! But Gabriel assured me that God had sent Michael and his angels, and they were literally surrounding our place."

(I would like to insert here that I used to be fearful when threats would come against my dad. I remember driving down the lane to his house one Monday evening, walking into the house with my husband, and absolutely getting goosebumps. I had never felt such a tremendous presence of God in that place before. I told my husband later as we were driving home, "Alan, I know that the angels were there tonight!" Alan agreed with me. He had felt the supernatural presence of God, too. The next day I asked my father if the angels had visited him the night before. It was then he shared with me that Michael the great archangel had been sent by the Father in the early hours of the morning the day before, and had set up protection around my father. The fear that had been generated in my heart by the threats against daddy totally disappeared. I knew that my father was protected by heaven's most powerful warring angel, as God's plan through my father, continued to unfold.)

"On two different occasions I have been told that God's plan before He ever made the earth was to take us to be with Him. Gabriel made this statement that although people fail to agree as to whether they go through the Great Tribulation, through half of it, or are raptured before, or don't believe in the Great Tribulation at all, when Jesus comes,

He is not going to look in people's minds to see what position they hold on this. He's just going to look in their hearts to see if He's living inside. Gabriel went on to say that it would be totally contrary to the character and nature of God for even one believer to go through even one day of the Great Tribulation time! Totally contrary!

"I will never forget an early morning hour in my family room when the giant warrior angel, Chrioni, was given permission by God to speak with me again. One of the things he told me was that 'Man will never fully comprehend the love of God!' He said that many of the people he and his hosts had been sent by the Spirit to help, had defied God. They had shaken their fist in God's face, and were filled with lawlessness and evil. Many were in satanism and witchcraft. They were God's enemies. But God said, 'Those people need help. Go and help them!'

"What can separate us from the love of God? We did nothing to earn it. So even if you are completely away from God and sentenced to hell because you haven't accepted Him, His love reaches out, and He says, 'I want you! I have room for you!'

"I see God now, like I have never seen Him before, and I feel that one of the purposes of these experiences has been for me to see God like He really is!

"I have been asked by people if I was permitted to ask an angel to talk to God in my behalf, or to convey a message through the angels to someone in heaven. I probably could ask, but I seem to be tongue-tied as far as asking very many questions are concerned. But God has given everyone of us an access to himself through Jesus! He doesn't ask us to go through an angel.

"I have also received a lot of letters from people asking me if it would be all right, or would they be violating the Lord in seeking an experience like this in speaking to an angel. I did ask Gabriel this question and the answer is so beautiful.

"Gabriel said, 'Tell men not to seek after an angel. An angel cannot hear your prayer. An angel cannot accept your worship. An angel cannot abide within you. But you have One within you greater than all the angels, and He asks for your prayers. He invites your worship and He will never leave you. So seek Him, Jesus!"

22
GOD CALLED HIM PASTOR

What is it like to be in the same family with a man who has actually talked with the angel of the Lord, Gabriel, and Michael, the great archangel? A man who has talked face to face with Jesus? My dad was a wonderful man, but he was very human. In fact the closer he got to heaven, the more his humanity seemed in evidence. He still loved to watch boxing, and we all used to smile watching our father enjoying boxing matches on TV. He would unconsciously jab and duck with the boxers in the ring. He enjoyed a good game of golf, although his busy schedule made it increasingly difficult to play. He loved sports on TV, especially football. Dad was very competitive and hated losing any kind of game, especially to his kids. Our family would joyously and loudly 'argue' different points of games with dad, knowing that we could never win the argument.

Toward the last, mom was alone a lot because of the urgency he felt to share the message God had given him. But even with his incredible schedule, they always had a lot of fun together, and were truly sweethearts. Dad was a relaxed Christian, who knew that God loved him as he was. He did not come across to anyone as a pious person. He was himself, and felt responsible to God and not to man for his ministry.

After having been a pastor for nearly thirty years in Boise, the people in the congregation had so many beautiful things to say about this man who was my father, it almost overwhelmed me. I would like to share some of the thoughts about him from his congregation.

Over and over again people mentioned his steadfastness, his terrific sense of humor, his compassion, his faith.

From several young people:

"He was my friend and pastor. His love and concern were as real as the love of my own father. When I expressed skepticism about the angelic visitations, he refused to argue or defend; he just told me to keep my eyes on Jesus, and he never became cold toward me because I had doubted."

"A deep voice behind me said, "Have you ever been baptized in 7-Up? That was the first time I met Pastor Buck. Although God was so evidently at work in his life in such an extraordinary way, he always enjoyed a good laugh."

From a day-care worker:

"The word 'pastor' is just a six-letter word until it is used in front of a godly man's name. Pastor Roland Buck was this kind of man. He always had time for you, and he always said, 'God cares for people.' I'm proud he was *my* pastor."

From his associate pastors:

"He was a man of high integrity, quick to respond when you were hurting, and sensitive to your feelings. He was a man ready to forgive and not too proud to ask forgiveness when the occasion arose."

"When I had to make a decision about marriage that broke my heart, pastor put his arm around my shoulder, and told God, 'Father, he's just like a son to me. Please let me carry some of the burden of sorrow that he is carrying, please let me help bear this load.' When I opened my eyes, big tears were streaming down his cheeks. This love and concern gave me a new picture of how God can use a willing vessel to bring His care to people."

"He took the words, 'I can't' out of my vocabulary and replaced it with 'I can, I can, I can!' He was the man most consistent in life and words that I ever met. He made God bigger to me than I had ever seen Him."

A member for twenty-seven years: "He taught us to be steady and sure, and to walk with confidence in God's love. He stayed on a steady course, never given to religious fads or new doctrines that sprang up in some areas."

From a marriage that was saved: "I called that 'Preacher Buck' at eleven o'clock at night. He didn't know me, but he told me to meet him at his office right away. He listened to me, and then he told me, 'I don't have any answers, but I know Someone who does!' My life was changed and my marriage put back together."

From a homosexual, one of many who found total deliverance as my father prayed: "As he prayed for me, I felt the power of God go through me so strongly, I couldn't move. Then I felt as though heavy chains had fallen off, chains I hadn't even been aware of. I was and am a brand new person. In Pastor Buck's eyes as well as God's, I am not an ex-homosexual, but a first-class citizen of the kingdom, made as though I had never sinned."

I realize that there are a lot of congregations who have beautiful pastors and who love them just as much as this congregation loved daddy, but I maintain that there was something special about him.

The next glimpse into my father's ministry confirms that very special uniqueness.

A young couple with several children visited the church and when they heard the beautiful message of reconciliation, their hearts responded. They made an appointment with my dad and accepted Jesus in his office. They told him that they had been living together and shared with him the desire of their hearts. He was absolutely delighted, and the very next Sunday night, my father entered the baptismal and told of the simple faith of this young couple. They had asked him to marry them, dedicate their two children, and then be baptized themselves. So standing in the baptismal, daddy did just that. The glow of God's glory flooded the sanctuary, and you know, I think if we could have peeked into the throne room, we would have seen a great big smile on God's face as He watched what was taking place.

I asked daddy once, "What do the angels call you when they talk with you?" With a voice that was husky and filled with feeling, my father answered, "They always call me pastor!"

My daddy was called by a lot of names. My mother called him "Sweetheart," we girls called him "daddy," my brother and my husband called him "dad," his other son-in-law called him "Pop," his grandchildren called him "Boppa," but God called him "Pastor."

23
NOT GUILTY

I knew beyond a shadow of a doubt that God had definitely spoken to me about writing this book about my father, but it wasn't until I began to go through his personal journal that I fully realized the responsibility the Lord had given me.

Daddy started keeping a personal journal describing the angelic visitations soon after they began in June, 1978. As I read the awe-inspiring accounts of these divine visits, my heart was thrilled. Then I saw why I was to write this book. In almost every account, the command is given by God through the angel, "Give this message to the world!"

The next chapters are taken directly from my father's journal just as he wrote them.

The following account of an angelic visitation is taken from my father's journal, dated June 30, 1979:

"As I muse over the way God has dealt with me during this past year through a constant awareness of His presence, and the daily reminders of His love by the Spirit, and the frequent visits by angelic beings, I am overwhelmed! I can't help but feel a sense of awe and wonder. Also a very real sense of responsibility. The truths He has revealed must be of tremendous importance to God to bring them by such extraordinary means.

"Again last Sunday, Gabriel and Chrioni came, this time dressed in the brightest garments I have ever seen. The material looked like spun gold. This was the first time I had seen Chrioni in anything other than his warring outfit. They directed me to the back yard where their brightness cast a dim, golden glow on the grass and water. I was spellbound.

"Sometime they may tell me why they were dressed like that. Could there have been a festival in heaven? Or did one of their assignments call for celebration? Or does God possibly give them a choice of garments? In any case, it was breathtaking.

"I was given another heavenly wafer and a drink of water by Gabriel. I burst out into a flowing praise and worship beyond my control." [NOTE: From *Angels on Assignment*, During a visit one night, Gabriel said that God had sent a round wafer approximately five inches in diameter and 5/8 inch thick, that looked like bread. He instructed me to eat it, so I did. It had the taste of honey. When I finished the bread, he gave me a silver-like ladle filled with what appeared to be water. I drank every drop of it, and an overwhelming desire to praise and worship God instantly came over me. Rivers of praise billowed up to God, bubbling up out of my innermost being, and for days after I drank this liquid, there was a sensation of "fizzing" inside of my veins. What an indescribably pleasant and exhilarating feeling it was!] (Daddy told me that the silver ladle was exquisite, with a beautiful design deeply etched into its surface.) "Again, a reaction took place in my body. A strange vibration. Charm felt it when she touched me. Instant miracles happened during ministry to those in need. This unique sensation lasted for several days.

"The message he brought from God's heart was concerning God's declaration that because of our acceptance of what Jesus has done, we are NOT GUILTY! Not only because of destroyed records, but because of a purged conscience (Heb. 9:13, 14).

"He asked that believers make the same declaration to

God, to themselves, to Satan, to others. Though their memories of guilt live on, the account written in the conscience is forever gone, and gives them peace."

24
TERRY LAW—THE CUTTING EDGE OF EVANGELISM

The following account of an angelic visitation is taken from daddy's journal, dated April 29, 1979:

"Early this morning I was awakened about 2:10 A.M. by voices downstairs. I dressed and went down, and as I suspected, Gabriel and his great companion were there. I will never get accustomed to the penetrating radiation that beams from them. Again, they had to restore my strength by their words and touch. What an exciting message from God's heart they had for me. After a few words of comfort, Gabriel seemed to speak direct words from God in the first person. 'The Lord speaks now to you. All your life forces are in me. Your drives, your talents, your skills, as you commit yourself, wholly, even your potential springs from me. Bring these words to the world. I have loved you, cared for you, yes, I have planned your steps, and when you would yield, have directed your path. Your successes come from me, your wealth has come from my hand. Your creative skills, your abilities to succeed are because of me. Because of your failure to recognize me and walk in my ways, you have limited the Lord your God, your lives have been restricted so that you have not known the potential of your life. As you make Him Lord of all, He will also be Lord of what you can be, not only of what your are (Exod. 31:1-6). Money and its power belong to the one who directs the use of it. Those who possess it. It is not a force apart from the one who controls it, Satan or God."

"As Terry Law was concerned about his future and the seeming peril of his work in darkened countries, he asked if I was permitted to enquire of God concerning these things. Normally, questions seem so trivial to ask, but God somehow let me know that it was all right. Here's His answer. "Terry Law has been chosen and prepared by God for a very special work, that of being in the forefront of His work in penetrating darkened countries with His life-giving light. The Father has interwoven a demanding urgency into all areas of his life. He has placed within him a persistence that refuses denial and a courage that accepts no defeat. God has opened to him long-closed doors, and has accompanied him by His Spirit. He is a chosen messenger. The Father has given him guidance and protection. He has provided for him in ways he has not known, by His Spirit, by men and by angels of the Lord. Though many have had a part in the preparing of this life, the turning point came as a young man under the Spirit-directed ministry of one of God's friends, Dwight McLoughlin."

Terry read from my dad's journal words used by God spoken through an angelic messenger to describe him, and his eyes filled with tears. It was overwhelming to see in writing what God had to say about him.

Alan and I were in Terry's hotel room. He had just flown in from Warsaw, Poland, for services here at Central Assembly. I had asked if I could interview him for this book because his name appeared in dad's journal, and also because of the involvement of our church in the ministry of Living Sound.

Alan and I spent an exciting two hours with Terry, as he shared with us confirmations of a tremendous breakthrough in his ministry with Living Sound, as dad had said would happen in the fall of 1979. We had just concluded our session when Terry read for himself what God had said.

Terry had many things to share, and Alan and I felt the blessing of the Lord so much as we talked, that here in essence, in Terry's own words, is our interview:

"I first met your dad in 1977 in a Mission's Convention here. Murray McCleese had been booked to speak but there was a conflict of dates, so Pastor Buck asked me to take over the conference as speaker.

"After the service, Pastor Buck drove me back to the Rodeway Inn. It was a dark, gloomy, rainy night. I remember sitting in his big brown Lincoln, and he began to tell me about his visit to the throne room. At that time he hadn't as yet had any angelic visits.

"He shared with me that when he came back from his visit to God's throne room, he was still holding the piece of paper God had given him with the list of 120 events that would happen either in his ministry, or in the world situation. He told me that some of the events on that list had already come to pass.

"I was so taken aback by this, that I didn't tell anyone, not even the members of Living Sound. The next night, pastor had supper with Joel Vasenen, the leader of the group, and myself. We sat there with our eyes bugging out because we had never heard anything like this in our entire lives.

"I was invited back to Boise in 1978 with Living Sound to appear with Little Richard in an "Up With Jesus" crusade in the football stadium. This time pastor began to outline for me some of the amazing things from his private conversation with the angels.

"Visiting the throne room is one thing, but talking to Gabriel is another. One of the things that the angel had said to him was that he and the church were going to have a direct ministry in the Soviet Union. Central Assembly raised the finances for us at that time for our first Russian ministry. I flew directly from Boise to Helsinki, Finland, and our team went into Russia for the first time. Pastor Buck considered that to be a fulfillment of one of the 120 items revealed to him.

"In 1978 I was here twice, and during these times pastor began to tell me the message of Gabriel, about the home, the atonement, and the importance of the blood.

"I did like Mary in the New Testament where it says, 'Mary heard all these things, and pondered them in her heart.' That's exactly what I did.

"Pastor Buck also told me that Living Sound was going to have a relationship with the Roman Catholic church. This was before the election of Pope John Paul II. We already had a relationship because of our ministry throughout Poland in 1976 with crowds up to 250,000 people. But Pastor Buck indicated to me that we were going to have a more intense relationship with the Roman Catholic church. I listened to what he said but didn't realize at that time that he had already been told by the Lord the name of the pope who would be elected. The Lord told him that this pope would be responsible for bringing unity to the fragmented body of Christ, which by the way, is the primary goal of the present pope. He, more than any other pope before him, has been accentuating the importance of bringing the entire church together.

"The introduction of Karol Wojtyla as pope in October literally blew me away because we knew him and had been in his home. He had talked with the group and loved the music. He even has our albums in the Vatican. I phoned Pastor Buck right after Karol had been elected, and he told me that he had known before hand. I remember sitting on a plane with him and he opened his diary and showed me the notation from 1977 when God took him to His throne room, and the name of the pope was number 113 on the list of events.

"In 1980 Living Sound and I were invited to an audience with the pope and had the opportunity to present a concert in St. Peters Square.

"The thing that shook me up the most regarding pastor's

angelic visitations happened in 1979. I had flown directly to Boise from Australia in April. Gordon Calmeyer was with me on that tour with Living Sound Team I. Gordon is the kind of person who says what he thinks. I had not shared with him a lot about pastor's visitations, because I had continued to ponder them in my heart.

"We were once again at the Rodeway Inn in the dining room. Pastor had shared with us for a while, when Gordon said, 'If the angels have said certain things about Living Sound and our relationship to your church already, next time they come, why don't you ask them about the future of Living Sound?' I looked at Gordon in shock and said, 'Gordon, you don't ask angels things like that!' Pastor Buck just looked pensive for a moment as though he were thinking, and then he said, 'Well, they can only say what the Lord has told them to say, but perhaps God will let me talk with them about Living Sound's ministry.'

"We dropped the subject and went on to something else. Later on in 1979 pastor had an appointment to be on the PTL Club. I was going to be there that same week anyway, so they phoned me and asked me to appear with him. I had a good time with him the night before we appeared on the show, but I hadn't had a chance to talk with him alone. The day of the program. I went into the makeup room and Paul Olson was there as co-host. Other than Paul, we were alone for the first time.

"Pastor looked at me and said, 'Terry, does the name Dwight McLoughlin mean anything to you?' My eyes opened wide, and I said, 'Yes it does. Why do you ask?' Then I said, 'Oh, no, you've been talking to the angels!' He just nodded his head. I asked him, 'What on earth did the angels say?' He said, 'Do you remember a time when you were a young man and received a call to the ministry?' I was dumbstruck. I didn't want to say anything. My mouth was hanging open. Pastor didn't go into that much detail except that he knew what had happened.

"From my standpoint, what happened was that I was a

thirteen-year-old boy. My parents were pastoring an Assembly of God church in Mount Vernon, a little town in British Columbia. I had gone to a camp meeting that summer on Vancouver Island. I had been deeply moved upon by the Holy Spirit in the service that night. When everybody else left the old tabernacle with the sawdust floor, the lights were turned off, and I was just sitting in the darkness praying.

"The camp evangelist, who was Dwight McLoughlin, had left his Bible on the pulpit and had come back to find it. He didn't know how to turn on the light, and was just trying to get to the pulpit.

"All of a sudden out of the darkness he called, 'Is anybody here?' I said, 'Yes.' He felt a sudden urge in the Spirit and walked down the pew to where I was seated, laid his hands on me and began to pray. As he prayed the Spirit of Prophecy came upon him, and he began to say things that shocked the daylights out of me.

"He said, 'Young man, I see you standing before tens of thousands of people proclaiming the gospel all over the world. I see a ministry to your generation that is going to be totally unprecedented in the history of the church thus far.'

"I began to tremble as the power of the Holy Spirit came on me. I knew I was hearing from God and yet it was a little bit more than my thirteen-year-old mind could take in.

"The next night Dwight McLoughlin called me up to the platform and announced to the entire audience of about 1500 people what I was going to do and be. He asked me to say something to the people, but I was hardly able to speak.

"I had almost forgotten the whole event. It was always in my subconscious, I'm sure, but when I walked into PTL and Pastor Buck mentioned that incident, I was absolutely overwhelmed.

"Pastor had been allowed to ask about Living Sound when the angels came to visit, but the answer hadn't come back about Living Sound. It had come back about me.

"The angel told pastor that before I was ever born God had a specific plan for my life, and an outreach that only I

161

was going to be able to accomplish. In other words, there was a sovereign call on Terry Law, that was distinctly for me.

"Gabriel told Pastor Buck to tell me that the struggles in my young life were ordained and planned by God to get me ready for the ministry.

"Gabriel went on to tell Pastor Buck that my ministry was directly ordained of God and that I would remain on the cutting edge of evangelism in areas where other people could not go. The angel said that the things I had gone through as a youngster prepared me for what was to come and the kind of head-butting I would have to do against people in communist countries who were violently opposed to the gospel that I would preach.

"Gabriel told Pastor Buck that these instances in my life were prepared by the angels. He didn't say exactly how the angels had organized them or been involved with them, but there had been a protective covering and preparation in my life.

"Pastor Buck said Gabriel told him there were two bands of ministering angels who traveled with our team and that is why we have not had accidents or difficulties with health. They have protected us during dangerous times in the midst of the Soviet World.

"Pastor began to tell me that the Living Sound was going to experience a breakthrough in our ministry at the end of the summer. I thought it was going to be in Red China because I had just been to Hong Kong, and some doors had begun to open for us there. But the breakthrough was in Russia. Pastor didn't specifically tell me what those open doors would be, but he mentioned that something unusual was going to happen. And it really did happen. We were able to schedule a 33-day tour in Russia and make major contacts with the underground. The ministry was tremendously successful.

"I felt impressed to come out before the end of the tour.

I had been traumatized in Russia by facing the officials, living on the razor's edge of danger, not being able to sleep at night, and meeting with the underground churches. I lived knowing that our rooms were bugged. We had to plan our services leaning over a balcony on the fifth floor with a KGB man below pointing a radar mike at us, listening to our whispers.

One of the hardest things I have ever gone through was getting a call from one of Central Assembly's board members at about two o'clock in the morning three days after I had returned home from Russia telling me that Pastor Buck had gone to be with the Lord.

"I was sick but I literally crawled out of bed, got on an airplane and flew to Boise. I wasn't strong, but I felt I had to come.

"Since that time, I've meditated a great deal on our experiences together. I don't feel that it was by accident that the Lord brought me in contact with Pastor Buck. The things the Lord revealed to him about me have been a reinforcement for me in my ministry, especially because I am constantly moving in the center of danger.

"I have a sense of assurance in my heart that there is a sovereign call on my life, verified by angelic visitation to Pastor Buck, and this has put me into overdrive. It has been a special experience for me. I know this is why God merged our paths. The Lord knew where I was and also knew that Pastor Buck would be a man who walked with God and be able to sense the call of God on me.

"Our whole friendship has been very sacred and special."

25
GOD KNOWS YOUR NAME

This is the account of daddy's last visitation by the angels before his death. The following is edited from the tape as he shared it with his congregation Sunday morning, October 14, 1979.

"I had an unusual experience that made me think about how much God cares for the individual. It has been about six weeks since I've had a visitation from the angels. If they never come again, I've had a greater experience than I ever deserved and the truths that God has made real have accomplished something so terrific. I feel like God has possibly given me all that I needed in the illumination of these messages, because God has given so many ways that He speaks. He speaks through His Word, He uses human beings as agents to answer needs, and He uses circumstances. Anyway, I never know from one time to the next whether or not it will be the last visit.

"Last night in my office, I found out that the visit six weeks ago wasn't the last one, because Gabriel and Chrioni came in. My head was down, and I was doing some meditating, and looking at the Scripture. They came in just like those people on the television series, "Star Trek." I was breathless because I never get accustomed to their presence.

164

"They were talking with me and gave me some beautiful truths about God's concern for the total person. Even our humanity is really a concern of God.

"Then the telephone rang. I let it ring for a few minutes, because I hated to be bothered with menial things like that while Gabriel was standing right there. I finally picked up the receiver, however, and it was a little lady from Sacramento. Her first question was, 'Have you seen any of them angels lately?'

"Then she told me that she had some needs, 'I've asked preachers to pray for me. I've asked friends to pray for me. Nobody seems to know how to get hold of God for me, and I don't even know if God knows about me. I'm seventy-nine years old and my husband is sick. Would you, the next time you see one of those angels, ask them to tell God that I really need some help?

"I said to her, 'Well, they're in here right now!'

"She choked a little bit, so I said, 'Do you want me to ask them? That isn't really their work, because you have the same kind of connection as they do to God.'

"She said, 'Please ask them.' I was going to turn and ask, not because I expected any answer, but Gabriel had been listening to the conversation. He evidently has a way of picking up the sound without it coming through the receiver. He told me that he heard what she said.

"He said, 'Tell Bonnie Thompson that God already knows her need, and He cares for her and loves her!'

"I told her, and she let out a squeal, 'He knows my name!' She hadn't told me who she was earlier, so I didn't know her name. She said, 'I don't care if I ever get this help, as long as I know God knows my name!'"

"This incident brought to my attention once again, that God knows my name, and He knows your name!

26
MORRIS PLOTTS,
A PRINCE WITH GOD

"I'm a hillbilly from Africa, and I'm here to see Pastor Buck the man who wrote the angel book!" I looked up to see who was speaking. He was very tall man with a beret on his head, a green plaid coat, and a yellow and red striped shirt. He had the biggest feet I had ever seen. They were size 16. "I'm Morris Plotts," the man continued picking up his big black suitcase which was covered with colorful travel stickers. I wasn't quite sure how to take this unusual looking "hillbilly," but I fell in love with the twinkle in his eyes, and I led him to meet my father.

There was an immediate rapport between the two men. Alan and I and our kids were excited when mom invited us to join them for dinner because as it turned out Morris shared with the family some of the wondrous ways God had led him through the years. One special highlight he shared was how twenty black African angels had helped him and his wife when their Land Rover was mired in deep, sticky African mud 200 miles from any known civilization. The story of Morris Plott's life is told in a book by Robert Paul Lamb and published by Jimmy Swaggart. It is entitled, *Bwana Tembo,*

A Prince With God. Bwana Tembo is Morris's African nickname meaning "Lord Elephant."

The following is from my dad's journal in which he kept the record of the angelic visitations.

"Early Sunday morning, July 29, I felt the warm presence of the Holy Spirit in my room. I obeyed the urge to dress and go downstairs for worship and meditation. Following a season of precious fellowship with God, I looked up to see God's messengers, Gabriel and Chrioni appearing in the room. Again I was overwhelmed by the divine glow and the holy atmosphere that surrounds them. They both took hold of my hands and I was strengthened.

"I was allowed again to behold the majesty of God. I saw Him in action caring for all creation, even the grass of the field. I saw Him caring for the animals. I saw reminders of Him in the clouds, lightning, and wind. I saw Him and His great love for man even those who have never known Him. This living panorama of truth is still alive in my mind. Oh, how Great Thou art, Oh, how much you love!

"Then as at other times, He gave me a reference. David saw the same picture and recorded it in Psalms, 102, 104, 105:1-5.

"He then introduced me to a ministering angel from Kenya, Africa, where God had released a large host to ready the people of that country for the Words of life. He stated that a prince with God who had been sent to this body, Morris Plotts, would be happily surprised to hear of the allies from heaven sent to aid him in giving his words life, and scattering the forces of darkness.

"This angel was black and dressed much like a westerner with casual coat and slacks. He was about 6'3", and of large frame. He explained that this host was active through-out the country. His personal assignment had been Nairobi, but he was ministering to a family in Msambweni, a city on the south coast of Kenya when he was directed to appear in Boise."

When daddy shared with his new friend how God saw him, Morris was overwhelmed. To be a prince with God is a wonderful thing. But everyone of us can be one of God's children. It is so easy, and God desires this so much!

God allowed Morris and my dad to have some precious time together when they met at Pastor Gorman's church in New Orleans, just one week before God called my daddy home.

When Morris returned to Africa, he found that what the angel had shared with daddy was true. Multitudes of Africans were finding Jesus as their personal Savior.

Morris was really excited when he and his good friend Louie Earl, a pastor from Plain Dealing, Louisiana, asked God to guide them to the family who the angel had been ministering to when he was directed to appear in Boise to meet with my dad. Pamela Berry, a translator for Evangel Translators headed by Syvelle Phillips was in Mombasa, Kenya. When Morris told her about the angelic visit to Msambweni, she begged them to take her along.

The town of Msambweni did not appear on any map, but Morris knew there was such a town because it was listed on an old African auto club directory, which he had kept for some reason through the years. He knew it was on the coast of East Africa because that's what God had said.

They stopped at a hamburger stand in Mombasa to ask directions and the African at the stand told them they were only twenty-six miles from Msambweni, and told them how to find it. As they drove down a road that was lined with coconut palms, a large sign suddenly came into view, anticipation flooded their hearts as they read, "MSAMBWENI!" As they drove into town, the first thing they spotted was a large government building. They parked and went in. In one of the offices was an African with a big smile. Morris began talking to him, and the man told him his name was Benjamin Mungai. He told Morris and Louie that he was one of the handful of Christians in the town. He said that he was the government official of "District Officer" in charge of the

110,000 people in his district, and 10,000 in the town.

Morris then proceeded to tell Benjamin about Pastor Buck in America, and the ministering angel from Africa who had visited him. He told Benjamin what the angel had said about ministering to a family on the coast of Kenya in the town of Msambweni. Benjamin began to really get excited, and asked Morris to give dates and places. When Morris told him, Benjamin was overjoyed. As Morris, Louie and Pamela listened with wonder, Benjamin told Morris how that so many good things had been happening to him and his wife he could hardly believe it. Seemingly out of the clear blue sky he had received a promotion. The town had gone through many government officials, but although Benjamin was a Christian, he had been able to carry out his government responsibilities very smoothly. He hadn't been able to understand this before!

Benjamin said, "Oh, my wife must hear about this!"

In the late afternoon, Morris, Louie and Pamela drove to the Mungai's home to tell the news to Benjamin's wife. As Morris stepped into their yard he had to pause for a moment in awe. The angel had told Pastor Buck that he had been in a home on the south coast of Kenya and this home was so close to the coast, the waves of the Indian Ocean were lapping the rocks in the front yard.

Morris shared the story with Benjamin's wife, and she sat entranced. Benjamin said, "All right, this is the first step, now what is next?" He then told Morris that there was a building right down the road he could have for meetings.

Morris couldn't accept the invitation at that time, but he is going back March 15, 1981, and packing a New Testament, written in Swahili, for every home in Msambweni.

Morris states: "Never, since I began preaching the gospel of the Lord Jesus fifty-six years ago, have I seen such hunger for God as I find in Africa today. A missions research organization finds that 16,000 people a day are turning to Christ in Africa!"

The following excerpt of a letter from Morris Plotts is an

exciting confirmation of the ministry of angels in Africa as shared with Pastor Buck by the angel Gabriel.

"Then while in the coastal area, I went down to Msambweni, the town the angel talked to your dear husband about. We sowed the place down with New Testaments in their own language. It has a population of 10,000 Mohammedans and I received a letter today from Dave Smith, our missionary there, and they are planning to start a work there *all because the angel of God visited my beloved friend, Roland Buck.* If you would be so kind as to do so, I would thank you to ask the church to pray that the hundreds of New Testaments we placed in the hands of these poor, benighted people will prepare the way for a great move of God there. They were so eager for the New Testaments, and to see them standing in the markets and in their yards with the New Testaments open and reading about the Redeemer from Heaven. . . . well, I will never forget that sight. When we were there, Dave Smith took my picture standing by the big sign with his little boy and two African pastors on the edge of town. The town itself is in the coconut grove about a quarter of a mile away. This is the town that was not on any road map you know. I am sending this to you to keep. I have one that I will prize and how I wish I could have shown it to Roland.

27
THE ALASKA ENCOUNTER

One of the things on the list of 120 events that were on the parchment that dad brought back with him from the throne room was a ministry in the Philippines. God miraculously worked this ministry out without my father pulling a single string trying to help God out. The complete story of Mission Philippines is told in *Angels on Assignment*.

I want to share a part of the story that is very special to me, because it shows the great love and compassion my father had for people.

When he arrived in the Philippines, he found that his time there had been very tightly scheduled. On the Monday after he arrived he met with one medical doctor, a college professor, and two pilots. They had just returned from Mindanao where there is a tribe which had been discovered just a year and a half previously. They were far back in the jungles, and while this group had been there, the professor was able to put together some type of a communication bridge to them. Daddy explained to them that God had sent him to the Philippines, and they said, "We came here for a rest, but we don't need it. Let's go back tomorrow. We want to take you down there because God is in this."

Daddy really got excited until he realized that it was

impossible for him to go because of his heavy schedule. That night he tossed and turned in his bed. It was hot and sticky in the place, and very difficult to sleep. Besides that, he kept thinking that he had really muffed it in allowing his schedule to be so tight. He pulled the sheets up in a big old knot, as he wrestled with this problem. About two o'clock in the morning, he finally went to sleep.

(I love this part!) About four in the morning, the light came on in his room, and he opened his eyes. Sitting on the other bed in the room were Gabriel and Chrioni. Daddy was so sleepy he said, "How did you find me here?"

Gabriel told dad that God wanted him to mingle with these people so they could get a good grip on this message and take it back to their area. This made daddy feel better, and then Gabriel said, "The reason we have come is that God has sensed the concern in your heart about your schedule. He wants us to tell you not to be concerned about your schedule, because it is so ordered and arranged that every person who meets with you has been personally selected by God to hear what you have to say.

This really relieved the pressure for my dad and he began to walk the streets and mingle with the people during the day, knowing that he was right in the middle of where God had placed him.

He saw a lady in the marketplace who was crying and crying, and through an interpreter, who just happened to start walking with him, asked her what was the matter. She said, that it was not important. Daddy told her that anything that was important to her was important to God. Then he prayed for her. As she lifted her head, it looked like the sun had come out in her face. She said, "Are you Jesus?" Daddy told her, "No, but I am His representative!"

He told me about a little old lady who was carrying a heavy load. He had been told that in this culture men never carry loads for the women, but daddy just couldn't stand to see her struggling along, so he took her heavy bundle and carried it for her. Word began to get around about this man who cared so much about people, and soon, everywhere daddy went, as he walked through the streets of the city, people followed him. He would stop and simply share with them the Good News. Many people were healed as they stood listening to him. Blind eyes were opened, deaf ears could hear, and the lame walked.

Before he left that city in the Philippines, the mayor of the city honored him with a special medallion.

It didn't surprise me, after he told me these beautiful stories of God's care in the Philippines that when he went to minister in Alaska Gabriel also found him there.

The following is the thrilling account of his Alaska encounter, in his own words, as he told it to our congregation.

"Early in the morning in Ketchikan, I heard the familiar voice of Gabriel. He told me not to get up, but to just go ahead and lie there. I'm sure he knew I really needed the rest. I hadn't slept over three hours any night while I was in Alaska, because of the tremendous surge of interest by the people, as we shared together following the services. The presence of God would be so close each morning I would get up in the early hours to just worship Him.

"The pastor's wife in Ketchikan was an Indian lady. She had seemed very happy as we visited around the table and in the home, but Gabriel said, 'I want you to bring a message to this pastor's wife. Tell her she is very special to God. She has a poor image of herself. She thinks she's worthless. She thinks that she's not accepted like she ought to be, because of her race, but tell her God loves her, and God has put her right where she belongs. Tell her she is special!'

"I could hardly wait to give her this message, but she didn't get up before I had to leave to catch my plane that morning. So, I told her husband. He told me that his wife needed this more than anything. I would have loved to have been a little mouse in the corner when he told her how God felt about her!" [AUTHOR'S NOTE: Two years later while I was compiling this book, I called this pastor's wife to hear in her own words her reaction to this personal message from

God. She told me she had been going through a tremendous crisis time in her life. . . . she really needed to know at that time God cared for her personally.]

"That morning, Gabriel also told me the name of a man God would use in a way of spreading these truths in areas I would never be able to touch. God prepares people long before they ever know Him. Gabriel did not say whether this man knew God or not, he just gave me his name, John Sandor. I wrote it down on my checkbook.

"Later when I got on the plane to fly home, I was really interested to see who would sit by me on the plane, just in case it might be the right one. So when a man came and sat down, I thought, "I wonder if this could be the guy." I was a little disappointed when he pulled out some papers, and I saw a name written quite large on them, and it wasn't John Sandor. I decided, however, that since he was sitting here God must have a reason, so I would tell him about the Lord anyway.

"I asked him, 'Would you be amazed or would it throw you if somebody told you that angels are appearing in the world today?' I went on to tell him the reason I was in Alaska was to bring the message that the angels had given me to share. He put his paper down, and listened very carefully to what I had to say. I told him how the Lord had given me names of several people ahead of time, and then I had met them on airplanes. He said 'That's really amazing!'

"He then told me that he was in forestry for Alaska, and that he knew the ins and outs and the little nooks and crannies of Alaska.

"We talked for a long time. I told him I also had the name of a man that I was going to meet sometime soon, who God was going to use in a very special way. He told me that this had been a very stimulating conversation. He asked me my name and I told him. Then he told me his name . . . John Sandor. When I let him know that his name was the one God had given me, he was really surprised. He told me that he never thought God would be interested like this in him."

[Author's note: I decided to try to give John Sandor a call. Sure enough, he was in forestry in Juneau, Alaska, and he remembered this meeting with my dad very well. He told me that it was very strange, because he doesn't talk with fellow passengers, as he is usually engrossed in paperwork. He told me when he told my father his name, he acted like he recognized it. This seemed odd to John, because his name is not a common one. Then my dad shared with him that God had given him his name through an angelic messenger, and there was more to their meeting than appeared on the surface. John Sandor told me this encounter with the supernatural had given him a strong reinforcement of God's care for the individual and that he could communicate with Him on a personal level.]

"Gabriel then began to share with me some further illumination about this message he had been bringing, and why the sacrifice of Jesus was so important.

"I hadn't realized before how closely associated to the sacrifice of Christ, was the function and ministry of Gabriel. I knew from the Scriptures he had previously given me, that he had been at Golgotha when Jesus died.

"He built upon the point again, telling me the tremendous need that people have of hearing the message: God has taken care of everything, and all their sins are covered.

"He then went into a description of the people in the Old Testament, as given by Paul in Hebrews 10:1-14. He was speaking about the sacrifices for the atonement that had to be made year after year. In those sacrifices, there was a remembrance made of sin every year.

"Gabriel then reminded me of when he stood before Zacharias in Luke 1. This was an example of the critical hour that took place when the sacrifice for the year had come to an end, and the next one was going to be made.

"During the time between the sacrifices, when the covering had expired, the people of Israel stood naked, hopeless, and helpless before the eyes of the eternal God. All the charges against them were under review by God. He saw their sins and their guilt as they were reviewed from year to year, and another year of probation had to be arranged (Lev. 23:27).

"Then Gabriel told me that he was present at every sacrifice for the atonement through the years, standing in the presence of God, whose position was above the altar in the Holy of Holies. Because Gabriel dwells in the presence of God, when God moved into the Holy of Holies, Gabriel moved with Him. He was unseen until he appeared to Zacharias in Luke 1:8-12,19.

"Gabriel said that the priest was offering up the incense, and the whole community was standing and trembling on the outside. Their acceptance by God was based on the observance of certain rules. They were making themselves acceptable during this interim period, when the covering had ceased, and before God accepted the new sacrifice. All the people were praying outside, because if something would have happened and the priest had not thrown in the incense (Lev. 16:12,13) he would have died, as there was no covering. Although he had prepared himself and made himself as perfect as he could possibly be made, he still could not perform his priestly duties without the covering. As the priest fulfilled this obligation, the cloud arose from the incense and covered him, and God could again smile because the sins were covered for another year. He smelled the sweet savor, and the stroke of His wrath struck the incense instead of the priest.

"God said to Gabriel, 'Gabriel, you can now appear in full view to Zacharias.' Zacharias looked and saw, standing at the right end of that altar, this giant angel. It scared him like it scared me. Gabriel didn't just walk in and stand there. He was present at every sacrifice through the centuries.

"Zacharias saw him and was troubled, fell, and fear came upon him, but the angel said unto him, 'Fear not, Zacharias, thy prayer is heard. I am Gabriel that stands in the presence of God, and I am sent to speak unto thee, and to show thee these glad tidings.' Every time Gabriel has appeared with a message throughout the Word, it has been with a message of 'good tidings.' And God is allowing him to be seen now, and it is still a message of 'good tidings.' The message is, 'The covering is complete!'

"The festival of atonement in the Old Testament was a reminder that Israel's probation had expired, and that their covering must be renewed. For this reason, man was given certain guidelines based on complete obedience so that they would earn a reprieve during the time of exposure.

"What God wants to say to people now, through His divine messenger is this . . . the sad thing that has happened in the lives of so many believers, is the feeling they are living, so to speak, in the hour between the sacrifices. And their acceptance by God is still based on what they are able to earn by the completeness of their achievement. Therefore, they are living in constant fear of making a mistake in the eyes of God.

"God said in Hebrews 10:12-14, through His servant, Paul, 'This man, after he had offered one sacrifice for sins forever, sat down on the right hand of God; From henceforth expecting till his enemies be made his footstool. For by one offering he hath perfected forever them that are sanctified.' The word sanctified means the sharing of His life. He has perfected forever those who share His life.

"I would like to share with you what Gabriel gave me about Jesus' sacrifice. 'As the fire of God's judgment struck Him, who was the sacrifice by the offering of himself, a cloud ascended that covered all time and space. It was carried on the wings of grace until it stretched backward across the ages to the beginning of man erasing all of those charges that kept coming up every year. It spread outward from Calvary across all ages to the end of time, completing a plan that was formed in God's heart before the world began, of making man acceptable in His sight.'

"Then Gabriel reminded me in a little postscript about those who sin and remove themselves from the covering through open rebellion and idolatry in their rejection of God as their leader and king. Hebrews 10:16. Those people place themselves in the same position under the blazing eye of God—open and exposed—as those Israelites were so long ago, during the interim period between the sacrifices. These people may look for other ways to try to produce their own acceptance through works, but there is no other way than to say, 'Jesus, I must accept the sacrifice that you made. I repent, and I am sorry for trying to go my own way. I come back!' Then the cloud will cover them, and they can be at peace again.

"This is the message that God wants the world to hear today. He wants people to know that the sacrifice is complete, and the covering is still there. It went out both directions through all the world, and then it moved through time until it reached our day. It will move on, continuing to cover those who have placed their faith in the sacrifice of Jesus, until the end of time. Jesus made one sacrifice for sin forever. This is a message of *hope* for all people who want to live for God."

28
FACE TO FACE

It was Monday morning, August 27. Daddy once again made his way down the hall to my office. With tears streaming down his cheeks he shared with me that the Sunday morning before, he had been taken to heaven to see Jesus for the very first time. He was still visibly shaken by this experience. He told me how he had been privileged to also meet with representative angels from every nation on earth. It literally took my breath away to listen to these words coming from my father's lips. I said, "Daddy, you have been to a heavenly staff meeting!"

The following Sunday he shared this awesome visit with our congregation. The following account is in my father's own words, as he told of his first meeting with Jesus, face to face!

"I mentioned last Sunday morning that I had received a very unusual experience right from God. I've had many, many people ask me if I would share it with the congregation, because you all feel like you have been made a part of what the Lord is doing. Last week I was almost dazed for part of the day, because it was something so real and so awesome. I know that I cannot convey the impact of this experience, but I'm going to read what I marked down, which is just a

179

brief outline of what happened. Again it portrays the great love of God in a way that I never, ever witnessed, although God has been letting me see each time, the greatness, the impact, and the weight, and the height, and the breadth of the love of God in ways that I hadn't seen in the past.

"I'm going to read this just the way that I have written it in the book in which I keep these things. There are several things that I will not be able to tell you. I have them written, but I've had to put big parentheses around them because of the instructions not to share them as yet.

"One of the most profound and inspiring encounters I have ever experienced occurred last Sunday morning, August 26, 1979. I was awakened about 1:00 A.M., and was ministered to by God through angels He had sent. In the course of this ministry, God allowed me to witness again His great plan in operation for making us acceptable in His sight.

"Coming alive before me was the message of Paul in Colossians 2:9-17, concerning the greatness of Jesus. He is the head of all God's forces. I saw the believer not only sharing in His life, but in His accomplishments fulfilling the law. His death, His resurrection is ours because of our faith in God's operation. I saw Him strip Satan of his authority and spoil him, never restoring it. He clothes us with confidence, and forgives every sin.

"Then something happened, and I was escorted into the presence of Jesus by these angels. I was literally translated into His presence. Like Paul, I am not sure if I was in body or spirit. It seemed like I was in body. I saw Jesus, met Him, talked with Him for the first time face to face. His appearance was identical to that described by John in Revelation 1:13-18. He appeared as the great judge of all. It is possible He will take on a different appearance upon His return. What I was allowed to see was His eternal appearance. His white hair hung to His shoulders. His face shown like pure white light. He wore a wide gold belt that was contoured to partially cover His chest. His shoes shown like polished copper. His eyes were much like those of Gabriel. Could it be that their garments and this appearance is characteristic of those who dwell in God's presence? My spirit leaped within me as He stated that His servants, these angels, had been sent forth to compel men and women to come to the point of choice. He made reference to the words that He himself had said . . . that which His angels said, 'there was still room.' He said to 'go out on the highways and the hedges and compel them to come in.' This is what He's doing now. God's last call to the feast. This is all because of the Father's great love for them.

"He also spoke of the numberless hosts sent into all the world to help prepare, and He used this term, 'the precious fruit of the earth for the harvest, the redeemed souls that He has purchased and prepared.'

"He then summoned representatives from every part of the world. I saw some ministering angels that had the appearance of Eskimos, who were working in the Arctic Circle. I saw some from different spots in the earth. Several of these I recognized as ministering angels I had previously met. There was one from Russia, who has been in my home three times. I saw Shaloma, the angel God brought to me from the Arab countries. I saw the ministering angel representing the multibillions of angels in Red China right now. There were many black angels. They were from India, from the islands of the sea, from all over. God has said that these were summoned from among the forces that have been sent out into every corner of the world and are preparing the harvest.

"Jesus stated that His purpose for this meeting was to remind me, and to remind the world, of the urgency and importance of linking arms with Him and telling the world that He really cares and telling the workers around the world that they are not alone. There are missionaries who feel like they're working alone, but Jesus wants them to know there are workers sent forth with sickles ready to work beside them in preparing the 'precious fruit of the earth' for the harvest.

"I am still not sure whether or not I was there in body, but it seemed like I was. When I returned I stood alone by the stream, almost like I was between two worlds. I was dazed, but more aware than ever that the countdown is nearly finished. The sickle has been thrust in. We must be alert, awake, full of faith, alive with His Spirit, and make each breath count for God.

"While in the presence of Jesus I was allowed to see the terrible days of tribulation ahead from God's viewpoint. I realize that there are many many different views and concepts about the tribulation, but I'm just telling you what God allowed me to see from His viewpoint. I can't tell you everything in detail, but from His viewpoint it's going to be a terrible time on this earth.

"I met with Gabriel's angels who have been assigned to these tasks. All of them were wearing the same type of garment that he wears, and will be extremely active during the Great Tribulation. God let me see at that time, and made reference that what I was looking at in this tremendous activity of angels was not something that He had assigned for them at that particular moment, but it was part of His great plan and purpose. We may not have been aware of it, but the angelic hosts—and I have discovered this in recent months—have been *just as active* when it hasn't been a time of tribulation. They have been active in God's great unfolding plan. This is just another phase of His plan. They have been active all along.

"I was allowed to visit briefly with Michael, who also has an important role to fill during that time. Jesus stated that even the Great Tribulation would not separate men and women from His love. That millions will be saved during that time by their own death, in standing for God in those days.

"He wanted me to carry the message to people who were discouraged and worried about their loved ones, wondering whether God really cared in bringing them as they were, refusing and rejecting. Some may feel at that time of the trumpet sound that many of these people have not made their start for God, but God's love still reaches them! They're going to seal their redemption by their own death during that time.

"They will die for their stand and be united at the resurrection, at the close of those days of sorrow, with their loved ones who have been taken in the rapture when He returns for those that are His. There's going to be a great reunion as God's great body moves out into the millennial days. Hallelujah!! Then He gave the reference, Revelation 7:9-16. John was allowed to see the same group of people. And John said to the angel, 'Who are these?' 'These are they who have by the sacrifice of their own life sealed their redemption.'

"The Holy Spirit isn't going to be totally gone, because the Spirit has seven different offices that He fills. His office for the church, *that phase* will be with us because He'll never leave us! But the Spirit of the Lord is still going to be working, fulfilling God's plan in another great phase of His work.

"These people who have heard but refused are going to be brought up short. I have preached many times that if you can't live for God now, you would never be able to in that day . . . but God said I was wrong. His love cannot be separated or destroyed even by tribulation! He let Paul see this and he described it in Romans 8: 'Shall tribulation separate you from the love of God? No!'

"This is not telling or encouraging men and women to go through those awful days of God's wrath. No, this is telling us that God loves people so much that He has made a plan for their rescue from this earth. Those that remember His Word and His promise and take their stand and let God know which side they're on. The tribulation is going to be a terrible time of the outpouring of God's wrath upon this world.

"People say that for God to be fair to others who have been in tribulation, all must suffer tribulation. He told me so lovingly, 'there's nothing we can earn by our suffering, nothing we can add to our salvation. We are saved because of the suffering of Jesus! *It would be totally contrary to the*

nature of God to cause His people to dwell in His wrath!'
He then reminded me of that beautiful Scripture in 1 Thessalonians 5:9, where He said, 'God hath not appointed us to wrath, but to obtain salvation by our Lord Jesus Christ.'

"He reminded me then of something that I didn't know before. That a little word spelled 'taken' used in Matthew 24, when He was speaking about this time, the Rapture, that one shall be taken and the other left. There are people that have said that this means the unbeliever taken in death. But what he told me is that God prepared a word for this usage only, not to be used again. Used only once in the entire Bible, and that word is the Greek word, *Paralambano** which means, 'called to one side in an affectionate manner.' And in that great calling, He is calling us as His bride to be with Him during that great joining of Christ to His church. 'Called to His side in an affectionate manner.' Then Jesus spoke to me and said that word was, 'Laid on the shelf, never to be used again.' I looked this up afterwards and it is true, it's used once. *Paralambano* if you care to look it up, you may. God said it, God did it. There's coming a time, real soon on God's calendar, it's almost here. I don't know how eternity relates to time but on God's calendar the countdown is almost finished. And He tells us that we are to comfort one another with these words. For a long time, I used to scare people half to death with these words. But I don't scare them half to death with these words anymore because the Lord has allowed me to see that there are three barriers that stand between man and God, and even if we got rid of every sin, we could still not approach Him because we still have human fault, human failure. But He said that by the covering of the Blood of Jesus Christ that sin is atoned for, that human fault is covered, that human failure is no longer there.

"He gave me a beautiful verse of Scripture, Colossians 1:22, where He said that because of the body of His death, we have been accepted, holy, unblameable and unreproveable in His sight. All three barriers are gone. When your faith

---

*"Although various forms of PARALAMBANO do occur in other places in the New Testament, the present indicative passive of PARALAMBANO (PARALAMBANETAI) occurs only in this passage which refers specifically to the coming of Jesus for His people."

is in the blood of Jesus, it's not your performance. For too long we have felt that our acceptance was based on our performance, but it isn't. It's based on His performance. When your faith is in what He has done, you are covered, whether you wake or whether you sleep you are the Lord's. You can live tomorrow with a song in your heart, not worried four or five times a day whether you're going to make it or not. Hoping Jesus comes during a revival meeting or that you die instantly during that meeting so you can finally be taken with Him. Oh, no! The Lord wants you to know that He has so much invested in you that He is going to protect that investment. And He's not going to let you out from under that covering without a lot of effort. This is what He said, 'That *man* had made it hard to get in and easy to get out, but that God's great plan was to make it easy to come in and hard to get out.' Hallelujah!"

I remember so vividly hearing this beautiful, liberating truth of God's love for man over and over again. It was literally burned into my dad's heart and ministry.

I read letter after letter from Christians who had been set free from the bondage of fear as they heard this truth. Christians who had been afraid to live a normal life, fearing they would stumble were radiant with new hope and purpose. They learned that God was not looking for ways to cast them aside. But instead, through the covering of the blood of Jesus, He has made provisions for plain every day down-to-earth living. Christians can relax and be full of joy, not anxiety.

Daddy also received innumerable letters and phone calls from people who had not accepted Jesus because they felt it would be impossible to live by the standard they thought was required. Thousands turned their lives to Jesus when they fully understood all God asked was that they place their faith in what Jesus had done. They realized nothing they could do would enable them to achieve the righteousness of Jesus so freely given to us when we believe.

Daddy shared with me several times, "Honey, this message surely must be important to God for Him to send it by Divine messenger!"

I close this chapter repeating this truth. God has made it easy for people to find Him and hard for us to get away from His great, overwhelming, matchless love.

29
NOVEMBER 6

This beautiful expressive letter to God was written by
Amy Gerla. She and her husband, Dan, had worked shoulder to shoulder with my parents for over fifteen years.

Dear God,

An oak toppled today, Lord; just like that! No big
storm, just instantly felled. God, how could it be? Oaks
live hundreds of years. There were no marks from the
blows of an adept woodsman. It was instantaneous . . .
JUST LIKE THAT!

You said, "He shall be like a tree planted by the water"
and he was . . . not just a run of the mill type tree like ash,
poplar, willow or yellow pine, susceptible to all sorts of
struggles with nature and swayed by every wind. But no,
he was solid, a mighty oak. Oh, yes, he'd suffered enough
in this life to give him marks of character, only to enhance
a life loved and respected by so many; he stood tall and
strong in the eyes of our family and friends and before
thousands of others.

We leaned on this tower of strength; probably more
than we realized. We could easily have lost our balance
but for You, Lord. You were here when that great tree
was uprooted, to be planted in that beautiful eternal place

where he is now basking in Your presence. I can just see him totally taken up with You! That's how he was here.

You've assured us that the same power, which kept that oak strong and erect through every storm . . . the person of Jesus Christ on whom he depended entirely, would remain with us forever. From Him we can continue to draw love, comfort, wisdom and strength.

Daddy was physically weary, but his spirit was invigorated when Alan and I and the children went out to the airport to pick him up when he returned from his speaking engagements in Louisiana. He had ministered with Pastor Ronsisvalle, a young pastor of a huge complex in Birmingham, Alabama. Daddy felt like the Lord really had His hand on this young man. He had found a true kindred spirit in Pastor Gorman from New Orleans. Daddy had laughingly told the congregation there that he had hit the top when he came to speak to them, and he didn't know where he could go from the New Orleans church. The frosting on the cake was spending several hours with Jimmy Swaggart. He told me later that he was thrilled as he sensed the warmth and humility in this man. He came back to Boise more stimulated than he had ever been before.

He was eagerly looking forward to ministering in Lakeland, Florida, with Rev. Carl Strader, and then going to Washington, D.C., to be with Rev. Benny Harris. Rev. Harris had made arrangements for every Senator, every Congressman, and every government leader to receive a copy of the book, *Angels on Assignment*.

My brother, Ted, and his wife, Linda, had gone to New York for their vacation, and were planning to meet daddy in Washington, D.C., to be with him during his meeting there.

It was a beautiful Fall morning, November 6. The sun was shining and the air was crisp outside. Inside, the atmosphere was electric with excitement. It was staff meeting day, and we could hardly wait to hear the reports of victory we knew dad would be sharing with us.

This particular day, daddy spent the majority of the time

talking about love and loving one another. He talked over and over again about how God had told him very specifically through the angel not to defend the message God had given him to share. He told us that it was God's message, and it was up to God to defend it. He urged all of us *just to love!* We were not to get angry at what people said about him, but we were to love those people. Love seemed so alive in his heart that day, a love that just oozed out of every pore. The supernatural love of God was so very evident in his life.

It seemed like daddy literally glowed with health as he ministered to all of us that morning. I was so glad because earlier I had told Alan that I hoped God wouldn't be lonesome for dad, and take him on a visit to heaven and not let him return.

Early that morning my grandfather, Arthur Jacobson, who had been ill for many years, had gone to be with the Lord. Arrangements had already been made for the funeral to be held after daddy returned from Washington, D.C.

After the staff meeting, I went to an ice skating lesson, and was planning to go to lunch with a friend. There was a delay in leaving the rink, which allowed Alan to reach me and tell me that my mother wanted the whole family to have lunch together.

Later I was so thankful to God for allowing me this last lunch with my dad!

Lunch was really fun. The family was sad that Grandpa Jacobson had died, but we all knew that he was with the Lord and released from the bonds of illness he had experienced for so long.

Everyone was laughing and talking at once. Mother's brother, Maurice, and sister-in-law, Margaret, were here because of Grandpa's illness. Marilyn was able to take time off from her job, and daddy was home from all his traveling. It seemed good to all be together. Marilyn was especially full of fun and really got daddy to laughing.

When it was time for dad to return to the office, Marilyn and I both gave him a big hug and kiss. Then mother, as always, sent him back to work with a goodbye hug and kiss, not knowing that this would be the last time she would see him alive.

Daddy had an appointment with a lady who hadn't been able to stop crying for several days. He prayed with her and then said, "I just want you to look up in the face of Jesus and give Him a great big smile, tell him how much you love Him!" She did and the tears turned to laughter which just bubbled out of her innermost being, as she began to praise the Lord. Then she looked at daddy. His head was back and his arms were relaxed on the chair. At first she thought he was praying and smiling up at the Lord too, but he was *so* still. Suddenly she realized that he was *too* still!

She quickly called Joyce, dad's secretary. Joyce screamed for Alan and told him pastor must have had a heart attack!

Alan shared later that when he ran into the room and saw him in that relaxed position, totally at peace, he knew in his spirit that daddy was gone. Alan laid him on the floor as a standard precaution and started giving him CPR. Sue Carpenter came in and assisted by giving simultaneous mouth-to-mouth resuscitation. Joyce called the emergency unit at the Fire Department.

I had stopped by Maranatha School and was talking with Warren Merkel who had been with Living Sound, and had just settled in Boise. I wanted to introduce Warren to my dad because dad's ministry had been so interwoven with Living Sound and Terry Law.

We were walking toward dad's office when Angela, my daughter, came running toward me crying, "Mommy, Mommy, Grandpa has had a heart attack!"

I said, "Honey, you're kidding!" but I knew that my daughter would never joke about something like that.

I ran to the church all the time praying, "Oh, God, don't let this be, at the peak of dad's beautiful ministry. Oh, God, please!" There lay my precious father on the floor like a fallen giant. Gentle hands led me from the room. It seemed like it took forever for the Fire Department to get there. I could hear people praying everywhere. Many of the students of Maranatha dropped to their knees where they stood to pray for their beloved pastor.

Mother arrived shortly with grandma, and Marilyn was close behind having driven top speed across town from her office. Marilyn came bursting in with tears streaming down her face. We all joined hands and hearts in prayer for dad.

The funeral home had already been called, but there was the very smallest sign of life on the emergency equipment, when it was turned all the way up, so the call was cancelled and an ambulance sent instead. The people prayed earnestly because they knew that daddy had been healed before.

The ambulance finally arrived and dad was rushed to the hospital followed by family, staff members, and friends.

The hospital was so flooded with calls as people became aware of what had happened that the switchboard became completely jammed. He had become such a well-known and beloved figure in the community.

Everyone was sitting in the waiting room praying when the door opened and the attending physician walked in. He went over to my mother, took her by the hand and said, "We did everything we could, but he's with God now! I want you to know that this man affected many lives, including mine!" The nurse who was there told how much she had been blessed by Pastor Buck. One of the nuns came over to me and enfolded me in her arms telling me that "Pastor had baptized me in water, and had enriched my life."

Mother was a beautiful tower of strength. She said, "Let's have a word of prayer together."

Mother shared later that she felt like every single day that she had daddy was a very special gift from God. She had made up her mind after his last heart attack that she was going to live every day with him to the fullest, but live it just one day at a time. The Lord gave her immediate peace and a sense of His presence the day she lost both her father and her husband of thirty-seven years.

"One of the things my husband spoke of often was that

God is righteous! He has the unfailing ability to always do the right thing! This helped me so much following the time when the Father called Roland home. How could I say 'Why God?' when I knew he was in the Father's hands all along."

The hospital had to send out a news release through the media to relieve their switchboard. Many of the congregation heard on television the news that their beloved pastor had gone to be with the Lord.

A special choir practice had already been scheduled for that Tuesday night. The musical for that year's Christmas presentation was based on a chapter out of my dad's book, "He Tasted Death." The program had been given to me in the middle of the night by the Lord, and daddy had been so excited about the presentation. There was no way to get word to all the choir members, so they came, many of them not knowing that their precious pastor had gone to be with the Lord.

Something really special took place that night. The people when they heard the news wanted to come to the church. They couldn't think of any place they would rather go. So that night as the choir came to practice, people started coming into the church until it was completely full. There was a beautiful spirit of praise and love. The strong foundation of trust in God that daddy had endeavored to build all these years was very evident as his people came quietly walking into their church and sat in the presence of the Lord the night my daddy went to be with God.

One of my dad's goals had been to see the mid-week service completely full of people praising God. The Wednesday following his death the church was full to the rafters. Many people came forward and shared what he had meant in their lives. It was wonderful. The congregation seemed to band together with a very special love and unity.

The Lord cares about his children so very much. His care was in evidence in His making sure that I was able to be at that last lunch with my dad.

My sister, Charm, was also included in God's comforting plan.

"I'll never forget the day when my little sister, Marilyn, called with the news that dad's heart had stopped. She said that he hadn't been breathing for about five or ten minutes. I felt like my heart quit beating. It was like when your legs turn to water.

"Bryan was working on the new building. My first feeling was panic. I felt like screaming, but I went out in the yard, and called Bryan over and I told him what had taken place. Through a miracle the Lord had worked out before, we were in Boise about twenty minutes after the family left the hospital. I believe it was a miracle the Lord performed to show how much He really cares for us.

"Our good friend, Naomi Fields, had been puttering in her home the evening before, and the Lord kept speaking to her to call and offer me and Bryan plane tickets to Boise because of my grandfather's illness. I didn't know how to respond, not realizing how sick grandpa was. I called dad after I finished talking to Naomi, and he said he really didn't think grandpa would make it through the night. That was my last opportunity to talk with dad on the phone, and I really praise the Lord for it.

"Naomi arranged for me and the children to fly to Boise the next day. When I found out that grandpa had passed away, and that dad wasn't going to be able to preach the funeral until the following Tuesday, we planned to cancel our tickets and go when the funeral was held. I thought I could be of more help then. In the meantime, I had packed suitcases for the family. Bryan's folks were at our house at the time, so when the call came about dad, I called the airport, changed our reservations, and Bryan and I were on the plane within forty-five minutes. We were home almost immediately after dad passed away. This was a real blessing to me."

Everyone was worried about Ted and his reaction to the

news since he was so far away from home. Ted had been so close to dad, and Linda had been totally adopted as a daughter by him and held a very special place in his heart as Ted's wife.

TED: "The last time I talked with my dad was Monday night, November 5. Linda and I were on vacation on the East Coast, and we had been alternating calling her folks, then mine, just to say, 'Hi,' and see what was going on.

"To give you an idea of the balance in dad's life, he wasn't an overgrown spirit, he was someone who was interested in things that were going on here, even with all the angelic visitations. The previous Saturday, Linda and I had given our tickets to the Bronco football game to dad, since we were going to be out of town. He had gone to the game with Sharon and Alan and watched Boise State play. Most of our last conversation was how much he enjoyed himself. He had watched the quarterback do a lot of passing, and it had been an exciting game. We shared for a while then I hung up, little realizing that this would be the last time I would talk to him on this earth.

"We were in Philadelphia. We had gone to see the Liberty Bell, and then had driven down to Washington, D.C. I said to Linda, 'Why don't we call your folks tonight since we called mine last night?' She called her mom and talked to her. Finally her mom said, 'Linda, there's something I have to tell you.' Linda hung up and turned to me with a strange look on her face. She said, 'Ted, your grandpa died this morning,' and without stopping she added softly, 'And your father had a heart attack and died this afternoon.' I looked at her with unbelief, and said, 'You mean dad's dead?' Dad was so full of life I could not picture him not walking on this earth. She said, 'Yes, we'd better call your mom.' It was as if I was numb for a second, and then I dialed the phone number. Alan answered and called mom to the phone. I asked her how she was, and then I told her that I had such a strange peace in my heart that shouldn't be there. It didn't make sense. But I knew where dad was and I felt a peace about it.

If there had been one thing in life that I really feared, it was when I would lose my father because of how much he had taught me and how much I had leaned on him. He was my earthly father and my spiritual leader, and he was gone! I felt a tranquility inside me like a storm had occurred in some way, but yet a calm came. There was no crying out, or striking out at God because I knew it had to be God's plan. I said, 'Linda, I need to go out for a while and do a little praying and talking to God.'

"I went out for about a half hour. As I was walking down a very busy street in Washington, D.C., I prayed, 'God, somehow I would like to be able to talk to dad.' Then I began to share just like I was talking to dad. Of course he didn't answer, but I thanked him for what he had meant in my life. I thanked him for the picture of God that he had shown me, for the time he had invested in me, for the heritage he had given me. I poured out my heart to him and let him know how much I loved him. I told dad that I didn't want him to be ashamed of how I conducted myself now that he was gone. Then I talked to the Lord about the church. The church was part of mom and dad. They had spent so many years pouring their very lives into it. I saw the church as a ripe plum to be picked by someone, not necessarily a bad person, but someone who saw it as a stepping stone, or a place to get away to, or maybe for someone a nice place to retire. Or maybe someone would come who would take the ministry that Pastor and Mrs. Buck had developed and turn it into a program.

"As I was out under the stars walking in the cool night air, cars were whizzing by, there was a frenzy of activity all around. In the midst of this noise in downtown Washington, D.C., I set my spiritual jaw. I began to think, 'What if God would let me take my father's place?' Then I thought about the fact that I didn't have any seminary training. I had attended the Roland Buck University for 28 1/2 years, though, and I began to wonder if there would be any way that I could be a pastor, although I didn't think I would be able to in my own strength. I went to bed still thinking about these things.

"We cut our vacation short, and the next day caught a plane home. I began to come back to reality and to realize that it would be very difficult for me to be able to be pastor of this church. I told Linda this, and she said, 'Ted, remember what your Dad always said, "If God is in something, it will happen with no strain or stress or human manipulation."'" We both were able to relax in this truth.

"By the time I got home, I had nearly resolved that there would be no way it would work for me to pastor. But I did determine that as a life-time member of this church, I would stand up and have a say in what occurred in the future.

"The day after we had arrived, mom and I were at the church talking, and Johnny Hisel, the senior deacon, came in. I told him that I would take a one-month leave of absence from my business, and work with my mom in the interim period. Three days later the board asked us to be co-pastors. I hadn't even thought about this but when I did, any hesitancy seemed to melt away because of my confidence in mom's spiritual maturity."

At home, our whole family moved in with mother. We all wanted to be just as close to each other as possible. The Lord wrapped mother in His love, and she emanated peace and serenity.

The board of the church met, and felt that daddy was the kind of man who would want the work of the Lord to keep going no matter what happened. They knew he would say, "Sic em! Life is for the living!" They felt very definitely led that all scheduled activities should go on as planned. Then something special took place. The board unanimously decided that there were no two people better qualified to take over the leadership of the church than my mother, Charm, and my brother, Ted. They would carry on the ministry the way it had been begun.

Ted had been one of the four owners of a new real estate company, Alpha and Omega Realty, which throughout the four years since its inception had become one of the largest real estate firms in Boise. There was not even a question in my brother's mind about quitting a successful career in real estate to become pastor of Central Assembly Christian Life Center.

The warm love of the congregation has been exhibited in their acceptance of my mother, "Pastor Charm," and my brother, "Pastor Ted."

30
CORONATION DAY

On Friday, November 9, there were two caskets in the front of the sanctuary of Central Assembly instead of one. But my mother had declared that this funeral was going to be a celebration time, a coronation day for daddy filled with triumph and victory!

And that's just what happened. God allowed that day to be beautiful with the sun shining and the sky bright blue.

Since there were going to be two services, one at 11:00 A.M. and the other at 1:00 P.M., many of the people took the entire day off from work. The first service was for Grandpa Jacobson. He had been ill for so long. He wasn't very well known in the church; but because of the people who took off work, there were about 500 people at his funeral. This was very special to grandma. Grandpa's service was blessed with honor and dignity.

Daddy's funeral was possibly the largest funeral that had been ever held in the State of Idaho with over 3500 people attending. Closed circuit TV was set up in the larger rooms so that people who couldn't get in the main sanctuary could still view the service. People flew in from all over the country. Telegrams came from hundreds of places around the country. Multitudes wrote to share how much they had been helped through daddy's ministry.

Mother asked the choir and band to sing and play several of daddy's favorite songs. One of the songs, entitled 'The Life Giver,' featured my brother, Ted, on the solo. My sister, Marilyn, was also featured on another favorite, 'Jesus the Resurrection.' Both of them received divine strength, and so did I as I directed the choir.

The presence of God was very real as dad's special brother, Reverend Walter Buck, stood up to preach the coronation message. The tribute that Uncle Walt paid to his brother through that message was so beautiful that I felt it needed to be included in this book about my father.

"I want you to know that this is holy ground. I do not feel worthy of untying my brother's shoes. I feel very honored at the privilege of standing here today. This platform has become a forum from which one of God's very good friends, and one of His most productive mouthpieces, has declared rich and supernaturally conceived, life-changing truths. You attest to that fact; this church full of people whose lives have been changed through the life and through the lips of this low key, unassuming brother of mine, husband of Charm, father of these beautiful young people who have blessed us.

"Through this beautiful man, God has chosen to touch not only an entire city, but far beyond the borders of this city. The influence of this life, through tapes, publications and platform ministry, across the length and breadth of this nation and around the world is awesome in its outreach. I know that we're not here to make people forget Jesus, for the very thing that epitomized my brother Roland, was the fact that he always wanted to stand aside, and let people see Jesus. We want to do that today, yet it is very difficult for us to talk about Jesus, without talking about Roland because they were very close. My brother's life was intertwined with the loveliness of Jesus Christ. I would like to say to you, dear friends, that Pastor Roland Buck was somebody extra special, not only to his family, his church, and his community, but I feel that he was very, very special to God. God had chosen to use my brother in such a way that those of us who knew him the best, had to stand in awe. It made me almost a little envious at times.

"I was captivated by a little sentence that Jimmy Swaggart printed in his magazine, *The Evangelist,* concerning Roland's tapes. 'I listened to the tapes with rapt attention, and a tremendous stirring in my heart. I sensed I was in the presence of Almighty God. This is a beautiful word from one of God's choice servants.' He continued to say, 'The things that happened in this life are probably one of the greatest miracles of the twentieth century!'

"Charles and Frances Hunter, who are here today, made this statement, 'With the boldness of faith we have never seen in anyone, Roland Buck has a total release of freedom in sharing what is happening in his own life.'

"My brother and I had the joy, a year and a half ago, of teaching the Spiritual Emphasis Week at Northwest College. We had a great time. The president of the school, Dewey Hearst, who is also here today, came out with a line that I thought was a classic concerning my brother. At the end of that meeting, he looked at the students and said, 'Young people, we've had two very different kinds of people here this week. One of these men has kept us on the edge of our seats, and the other one has kept us on the edge of eternity.'

You know why my brother was keeping people on the edge of eternity? That's where he lived! He was living in two worlds at the same time. He just got closer to the other world than this world, and God said, 'There's no point in your going back!'

"I was at my brother's home this morning, and the phone rang. Everybody was busy, so I answered it. It was a lady calling from Marion, Ohio. She said, 'Is Brother Buck there?' I said, 'Well, I'm Brother Buck, but I don't think I'm the one you're looking for.' I've been saying this now for the past year, and I just want you to know I'm happy to take that position, praise God! I told this lady that Roland had been promoted and that he's in another phase of a terrific ministry, and that we were going to have a memorial service for him today. She said, 'I read his book last night, and it changed my life!' This is happening again, and again, and again!

"I know what is going through some of our minds if we're not totally tuned in. We say, 'Well, Pastor Buck was arriving at the very peak of his efficiency, what could God possibly have in mind taking Pastor Buck away from all of this tremendous acceptance? No doubt there could have been other books, and great auditorium meetings.' The human reaction would be to say, 'What a waste! Only sixty-one years of age.'

"Well, I would say, away with that nonsense about waste, dear friends. I feel that the cycle had been completed, and what happened to my brother, Roland, is what should have happened. You say, 'That's crazy!' No, God is perfect in His timing. My brother lived right up to the 'enth' degree until the Lord took him home. He was sitting in his office sharing Jesus with a lady. She was delivered. She was rejoicing in the Lord. He told her, 'Why don't you just look up now, and smile at Jesus.' Then he sat back and smiled, and his two angel friends came and said, 'Now come on, let's get on to phase two!'

"The book has been written and is well launched. The message is girding the globe. The plan is complete as far as this phase of life is concerned, and Roland on Tuesday afternoon, went on to God's next development.

"I would like to say that I'm so delighted that before the Lord took him home, Roland received from his peers the recognition that was long overdue. Roland served in a rather quiet place for many years just doing his thing. And I'm thankful that the world finally discovered your pastor. God knew about him all the time. But he suddenly pulled the curtain aside, and a ministry evolved and was revealed that touched the multitudes.

"I mingled around your foyer for about thirty or forty minutes today, and I didn't find very many defeated people. I

201

feel that there's not very much gloom in the camp, because God doeth all things well! He's on the throne!

"Our hearts ache, because we're human. I think there's room for tears. We would be less than human if there were no tears. God made us so we could cry. That's a wholesome thing. It's a cleansing for the soul. When we think of the empty chair, and the pulpit. When we think of the unoccupied counseling room, the shock of bereavement, as we meditate on the suddenness of his going, there are going to be some moments when we're going to hurt. I hurt, because Roland and I were not only brothers, we were good friends. I have lost a friend as well as a brother. I have lost a confidant. I have lost a man whom I tried almost everything I ever did on for size to see how he would react. He reacted violently to some of the things I tried on him incidentally.

"When we think objectively, we rise above this human reasoning, and we see the wonderful pattern of God for His children. I read in Psalms 116:15, "Precious in the sight of the Lord is the death of his saints." This doesn't mean that God is anxious to end the life of those who serve Him. The word precious means that He places a high value on them. He will suffer none of those who are living close to Him to die needlessly. In fact, so precious is their death, that He watches over them every moment of every day to prevent it! We are living, not charmed lives, but immortal lives until our work is done. I feel that Pastor Buck was immortal until his work was done, and then He moved into Glorious Eternal Immortality.

"Roland was so steady, strong, and stable that we kind of thought that if anything happens we can put another tube in and he'll just go on forever. But our times are in God's hands, and Roland's times were in His hands. God had scheduled every moment of Roland's life. He knew all about Tuesday of this week, years and years ago.

"When we walk with Christ and we're led by His Spirit, when we possess His Life, until our appointed time comes, we can say to epidemic, or danger, or to whatever would cast a shadow on our lives, 'You have no power against me except it was given you of God!'

"I asked Roland one day, 'How in the world do you keep going like you do?' He said, 'Well, the Lord kind of moved my heart over to one side, and connected me with His big heart.' I believe that too!

"I was in the Evangel Bookstore in Spokane, and one by one all the personnel of that store who have met Roland, and loved him, came by and said that they were sorry, and hurt with me. I thanked each one of them, as they came. While they were coming and talking with me, right beside me was a table stacked with 200 books entitled, *Angels on Assignment,* the Holy Spirit whispered to me that 'Though he is dead, in our human parlance, yet he speaketh!'

"And Roland's voice is being heard again, and again, and again. You know the word the Holy Spirit dropped in my heart was that his ministry, rather than dying, is exploding, and only God knows the end result.

"For twenty years Roland served his church. It was a good normal growth. God's presence was real; people found the Lord. But then something really happened. All the time there were indications of a special supernatural touch.

"I remember one time in your old building, on a Sunday, when I preached for Rol. He nudged me and said, 'See that couple over there? Remind me to tell you about them after church.' God had revealed these people to him before the service one morning. He told Roland to 'Go to the foyer, they're coming in about now, so go meet them and bring them in your office. They're ready right now to accept Jesus.' My brother met these people, and took them in the office, and led them to the Lord. He said, 'I walked into my pulpit ten feet tall that morning, realizing that I wasn't doing this alone, but God cares about people.' That was the theme of his life.

"I encourage you, dear friends, if you haven't met Christ, I know what Roland would want you to do. His whole life was lived to touch people and bring them into the kingdom. I challenge you to make sure that you are keeping eternal values in view."

At the close of my uncle's remarks, the Singing Ambassadors once again sang the beautiful song of victory, "The Hallelujah Chorus." The choir was more anointed this time than they were when they had sung it the year before for the heavenly visitor. I personally felt the presence of God in the place, and I felt that thousands of angels attended my father's coronation service.

Usually when a funeral service is over, the people file by the casket, and the family is the last, after everyone else has gone.

My mother shares: "As the last strains of the 'Hallelujah Chorus' ended in a note of triumph, the casket was opened and it was time for our precious people to say goodbye to their pastor and friend. I realized that they were like sheep without their shepherd. They needed comfort and encouragement. So I stood to my feet, walked over to stand beside my brother-in-law, Walter Buck, who had ministered. Then my children came and stood with me. As our congregation, friends from the neighborhood and around the nation, and those who had been helped by Pastor Buck walked by, we shared in mutual sorrow and the Lord Jesus wrapped us in His love."

Many people were challenged that morning to help carry on the message of how much God loves people, and to share the importance of the sacrifice of Jesus.

We heard some people say, "We have lost Pastor Buck!" The answer comes ringing back loud and clear, "We haven't lost Pastor Buck. We know right where he is!"

EPILOGUE
WHAT'S HAPPENING
TO THE MESSAGE?

The Sunday following coronation day, my brother, the new Pastor Ted Buck, stepped up to the pulpit for the very first time in this capacity. He was twenty-eight years old and he looked very young.

The church was so packed with people, the overflow area had to be opened. Those who thought they had time to play around, but would some day accept the Lord into their lives, came to Jesus by the hundreds after my father's death.

The night before Ted's first service as pastor, he went to my dad's office.

"There had been a lot of activity going on. The coronation service had been the day before, then there had been a wedding, so by the time I finally had some time to myself, it was 11:00 P.M.

"I began to pray and think 'How can I step into the pulpit of a man who had ministered for forty years, pastored this church for almost thirty years, who had talked with angels, and who had walked so closely with God? He had talked face-to-face with Jesus Christ? Here I am, an accounting major, in business for 5½ years, how in the world can I step into the shoes of a man like this?'

"I knew that I didn't feel any sense of competition with

dad. I was his biggest supporter. No one thinks more of him than I do, unless it would be the Lord or mom.

"I was really nervous about how I was going to step into the pulpit of a man like that.

"As I sat in his big chair, where he had been visited numerous times by angels, I looked around, but they weren't there. I began to open my heart up to God asking Him for help. He flooded my heart with His presence, a very special presence. It was not a unique experience like an angelic visitation, but it was God saying to me, 'I'm here!' At that point I felt confidence burning in my heart because God had met me, and I had something to say. I knew beyond a shadow of a doubt that this was my destiny. No man had placed me there, but God had chosen me to be the pastor of Central Assembly Christian Life Center."

My mother, "Pastor Charm," had been working in a supportive role all through the years of dad's ministry, although she had been a pastor when they were married.

When she was appointed co-pastor of our thriving church, she too, received a tremendous anointing of the Holy Spirit. My mother has had the opportunity to travel all over the country continuing to share the message of God's love.

The church family has rallied, and there has not been one low Sunday. Instead, the throngs of people coming to the church have added to the growing pains of an already taxed facility.

People continue to be saved every week. God continues to work miracles of healing and changing lives. Marriages are being put back together. Calls continue to come in from all over the world from people whose lives have been touched through God's obedient servant, my father, Pastor Roland H. Buck.

The Wednesday before daddy went to be with the Lord, he shared with the people in his Bible study that he would like his grave marker to read, "Roland Buck, He inspired the faith of others." My father truly reached his goal.

AFTERWORD
HAVE YOU CONFIRMED
YOUR RESERVATION?

I have shared through the pages of this book the true story of a man I knew very well as my father, my pastor, and my boss. I have tried to give you a glimpse of his great sense of humor and his down-to-earth humanity. I have wanted to share with you a man, who although very special, was still just an ordinary man. However, of utmost importance is the way this special, yet ordinary man was unique in the way that he walked with God.

Dr. Hurst, president of Northwest College wrote in the Northwesterner, "One of the classic statements of Scripture was said of Enoch, "He walked with God, and was not for God took him." For those who knew the late Reverend Buck the same statement could be said of him. He walked with God . . . God took him. Roland was more than a champion of the supernatural, he was a channel. Perhaps no greater tribute can be paid to Roland Buck than this. He was an ordinary man who believed God and walked with God. Through his life and ministry God has brought to himself multitudes of men He has purposed to save."

The message that was given to my father by angelic messenger continues to reach out and touch lives today. Perhaps this message of God's love has touched you and made you aware of what God is really like!

One of dad's favorite sermonettes was that God planned for everyone to spend eternity with Him. He is not willing that any should perish. When a person is born, his name is written in God's Big Book, and is not removed until he or she dies without accepting what Christ has done.

Daddy used to say that Jesus reserved a place for everyone in heaven by His sacrifice at Calvary, but it's up to each individual to confirm, or pick up that reservation that Christ made for them.

If you haven't already "confirmed your reservation", why not confirm it right now? Just pray this simple prayer.

"Father, I accept what Jesus has done for me by His death on the Cross. I invite you into my life right now. Forgive all my sins. Thank you Jesus."

Now, no matter where you are coming from, or how bad you feel you have been, at this moment in God's eyes, you are as clean and pure as a new born baby. You are innocent, and made as though you had never ever sinned. Praise the Lord!

Daddy always told people after they had "confirmed their reservations"—"Just like pounding a nail in a board, you clinch it by bending the nail over on the other side!" He had people clinch what had happened to them by calling someone and letting them know what Jesus had done for them. If you have accepted Jesus in your life for the first time, or renewed your dedication to Him, why not clinch it, by calling someone and letting them rejoice with you in what Jesus has done.

Now, why not do one more thing. I would love to hear from you how the message of God's love and care touched your life. Why not drop a note in the mail to me.

Now, begin reading your Bible and be sure to find one that's easy for you to understand. The main purpose of the Bible is to show us what God is like. It will really help you get to know Him.

And then find a good church where the Bible is taught.

Worship and fellowship with other Christians will help you tremendously in your walk with Christ.

Thank you for letting this beautiful message of God's love and care touch your life.

ANGELS ON ASSIGNMENT (Hunter Books)
BY ROLAND H. BUCK

US Funds $5.00 (Includes postage and handling.)
Order from: HEARTBEAT MINISTRIES
            BOX 4006
            BOISE, IDAHO 83704 USA
For additional copies of "The Man Who Talked With Angels"
send $7.00 US Funds

TAPES BY PASTOR ROLAND H. BUCK

I. **TWO TAPES RELATING TO AN UNUSUAL EXPERIENCE IN PASTOR BUCK'S LIFE WHERE GOD ALLOWED HIM TO BE LIFTED IN THE HEAVENLIES FOR A BRIEF VISIT.**

   1. I VISITED THE THRONE ROOM
      (I visited the Throne Room on January 21, 1977. A unique experience of being lifted into the very presence of God and receiving a manuscript containing glimpses of many things to come.)

   2. SEQUEL TO THE THRONE ROOM
      (DEC. 1978 . . . a later look at the events predicted in the visit to the Throne Room and their fulfillment.)

II. TAPES OF ANGELIC ENCOUNTER ... by Pastor R.H. Buck

1. GOOD NEWS FOR YOU AND YOUR FAMILY
   (God's plan of hastening the believer's loved ones to a point of choice.)

2. WHEN GOD SAYS, "THANKS"
   (The believer's judgement . . . a day in which God has chosen to say "Thanks".)

3. MINISTRY OF ANGELS
   (A first hand description of Angelic beings in action.)

4. ANGELS ON ASSIGNMENT
   (The exaltation of Jesus by Angelic beings . . . a close look at Angelic beings in action.)

5. HE TASTED DEATH
   (In Jesus' death, the stroke of God's wrath was diverted from man to Himself.)

6. DISCERNING HIS BODY
   (Words brought by Angelic messenger concerning the power and purpose of Communion.)

7. WHY GOD?
   (Divine answers to questions that plague believers.)

8. THE ZEAL OF THE LORD
   (God hath promised . . . He is able to perform. . . He will finish what He started.)

9. MICHAEL AND HIS ANGELS
   (The awesome appearance of Michael and his angels and their message of hope.)

10. SELECTED FOR THIS HOUR
(A challenge to each individual to bring their life to its highest purpose.)

11. THIS IS OUR DAY #1
(Truths brought to us by Divine Messengers (Angel) indicates to us that these days are very special.)

12. THIS IS OUR DAY #2
(Not only a time of lawlessness, but the greatest of all days for the believers. Also includes the account of Michael's appearance.)

13. WHAT LIES AHEAD
(A look at God's plan for His body in this day.)

14. WHAT IS GOD DOING?
(A message on God's intent and purpose today.)

15. HE IS COMING AGAIN
(God's Priorities" . . . a reminder of the nearness of Christ's return and His message for this hour.)

16. GOD WANTS YOU TO KNOW
(Concerns things important to God . . . including a glimpse of believers who have gone before . . . clothed with their heavenly bodies.)

17. JESUS LORD OF ALL
(Includes exciting Angelic experience.)

18. READY TO GO
(The rapture - creation of man? or God?)

19. THE POWER OF HIS WORD
(The place and purpose of experience in the believer's life.)

20. NOT GUILTY
(God's declaration concerning you.)

III. SELECT MESSAGES . . . by Pastor R.H. Buck

1. YOUR POTENTIAL AND GOD
("The dual message of Grace" . . . a message on the believer's responsibility to reflect the beauty of Jesus. "God's desire is the believer's potential and should be His good.")

2. MISSION PHILIPPINES
(A recurrence of the Acts experience.)

3. WHAT IS NORMAL FOR THE BELIEVER
(God's norm for His body as seen in the New Testament Church.)

4. PORTRAIT OF GOD (set of FOUR tapes)
(Many of the problems of the believer are the results of a wrong view of God. In these four messages you will take a look at God as He really is.)

5. GOD'S PRIVILEGED LIST
(You too can find favor with God.)

6. ANGEL'S FOOD
(God's cure for boredom in the believer's life.)

7. RELIGION OR RELATIONSHIP
(God's offer to man is more than another relationship, but the joining of His family.)

8. THE NEW TESTAMENT CHURCH LIVES AGAIN
(An answer to the teaching that the day of miracles is past.)

9. GOD'S OPEN DOOR
(God's highest interest in restoring man to a place of fellowship is proven by continually presenting opportunities to find Him.)

10. STREAMS IN THE DESERT
(A place of refreshing in those dry places of life.)

11. DIVINE BREAKTHROUGH

12. GOD OF THE VALLEY
(Not only is He God in good times, but has proven He is God of your valley.)

13. MEN OF DESTINY
(Things do not "just happen" in God's economy . . . not only is the future planned, but men are chosen for these plans.)

14. THE NEWS IS GOOD
(Jehovah reigns . . . "Let the nations rejoice.")

15. LISTEN, HE CALLS YOUR NAME
(A message on God's personal interest in each individual.)

16. FROM GOD'S POINT OF VIEW
(The impotence of witchcraft.)

IV. CURRENT MESSAGES . . . by Pastor R.H. Buck

1. DAY APPOINTED
(The unerring accuracy of God's plan.)

2. GOD'S WARNING SIGNALS
(A Bible warning against presuming on the grace of God.)

3. WHAT MEANETH THIS
(Bible answers to the oft asked questions regarding supernatural happenings.)

V. LATER MESSAGES WHICH INCLUDE ANGELIC REFERENCE

1. COUNTDOWN
(A close look at God's time line of the ages.)

2. DISCOVERING YOUR POTENTIAL
(Every drive, every life force planted within man is by God.)

3. ACTION IN HEAVEN
(A look away from earth's problems to the stepped up activities of Heaven.)

4. LEST WE FORGET
(Includes a glimpse into God's treasure chest of memories.)

5. THAT YOU MIGHT KNOW
(Assurance that this Angelic visitation is of God.)

6. WORLD AFLAME
(Confirmation of God's Promise to accompany these words and give them life.)

7. ANSWERS TO QUESTIONS YOU HAVE ASKED
(Answers to several main questions that have been asked since Pastor's book was published.)

8. GOD'S GOLDEN KEYS (set of 8 tapes)

9. PILLARS OF ETERNITY
(Last 3 sermons by Pastor R.H. Buck)

10. PASTORS CORONATION SERVICE
(Victorious Funeral Service for Pastor R.H. Buck,
Nov. 9th, 1979.)

11. VISITATIONS OVERVIEW
(Taped in New Orleans Oct., 1979, Pastor Buck
giving general overview of Angelic visitations.)

ALL TAPES $4.00 ea. (U.S. Funds)
(includes postage and handling.)
4th Class Special (Foreign add $2.00 U.S. Funds)

ORDER FROM:
Heartbeat Ministries
Box 4006
Boise, Idaho 83704 USA

FREE BOOK CATALOG INSPIRATIONAL BOOKS

Support your local Christian Book Store
Send for free catalog of books-Bibles-cassettes
Write; IPSI-Catalog
　　　Box 146
　　　Mendham, N.J. 07945